How to Know the Ferns

A GUIDE

TO THE NAMES, HAUNTS, AND HABITS OF
OUR COMMON FERNS

By

Frances Theodora Parsons

Author of "How to Know the Wild Flowers,"
"According to Season," etc.

Illustrated by

Marion Satterlee and Alice Josephine Smith

SECOND EDITION

Dover Publications, Inc.
New York

Published in Canada by General Publishing
Company, Ltd., 30 Lesmill Road, Don Mills,
Toronto, Ontario.
Published in the United Kingdom by Constable
and Company, Ltd., 10 Orange Street, London
WC 2.

This Dover edition, first published in 1961, is an
unaltered republication of the original work with
the omission of six photographic illustrations. These
illustrations contributed little to the value of the
work and were omitted because of their poor
quality. The work was originally published by
Charles Scribner's Sons in 1899.

Standard Book Number: 486-20740-4
Library of Congress Catalog Card Number: 61-1261

Manufactured in the United States of America
Dover Publications, Inc.
180 Varick Street
New York, N. Y. 10014

TO

J. R. P.

"If it were required to know the position of the fruit-dots or the character of the indusium, nothing could be easier than to ascertain it; but if it is required that you be affected by ferns, that they amount to anything, signify anything to you, that they be another sacred scripture and revelation to you, helping to redeem your life, this end is not so easily accomplished."

—THOREAU

PREFACE

Since the publication, six years ago, of "How to Know the Wild Flowers," I have received such convincing testimony of the eagerness of nature-lovers of all ages and conditions to familiarize themselves with the inhabitants of our woods and fields, and so many assurances of the joy which such a familiarity affords, that I have prepared this companion volume on "How to Know the Ferns." It has been my experience that the world of delight which opens before us when we are admitted into some sort of intimacy with our companions other than human is enlarged with each new society into which we win our way.

It seems strange that the abundance of ferns everywhere has not aroused more curiosity as to their names, haunts, and habits. Add to this abundance the incentive to their study afforded by the fact that owing to the comparatively small number of species we can familiarize ourselves with a large proportion of our native ferns during a single summer, and it is still more surprising that so few efforts have been made to bring them within easy reach of the public.

I wish to acknowledge my indebtedness to the many books on our native ferns which I have consulted, but more especially to Gray's " Manual," to Eaton's " Ferns of North America," to the " Illustrated Flora " of Messrs. Britton and Brown, to Mr. Underwood's " Our Native Ferns," to Mr. Williamson's " Ferns of Kentucky," to Mr. Dodge's " Ferns and Fern Allies of New England," and to that excellent little quarterly, which I recommend heartily to all fern-lovers, the " Fern Bulletin," edited by Mr. Clute.

To the State Botanist, Dr. Charles H. Peck, who has kindly read the proof-sheets of this book, I am indebted for many suggestions; also to Mr. Arthur G. Clement, of the University of the State of New York.

To Miss Marion Satterlee thanks are due not only for many suggestions, but also for the descriptions of the Woodwardias.

The pen-and-ink illustrations are all from original drawings by Miss Satterlee and Miss Alice Josephine Smith.

In almost all cases I have followed the nomencla-
ture of Gray's "Manual" as being the one which
would be familiar to the majority of my readers,
giving in parentheses that used in the "Illustrated
Flora" of Messrs. Britton and Brown.

FRANCES THEODORA PARSONS

ALBANY, March 6, 1899

" The more thou learnest to know and to enjoy, the more full and complete will be for thee the delight of living."

CONTENTS

CONTENTS

LIST OF PLATES

LIST OF PLATES

LIST OF ILLUSTRATIONS

LIST OF ILLUSTRATIONS

How to Know the Ferns

New York Fern

— FERNS AS A HOBBY

I THINK it is Charles Lamb who says that every
man should have a hobby, if it be nothing better
than collecting strings. A man with a hobby turns
to account the spare moments. A holiday is a delight instead of a bore to a man with a hobby.
Thrown out of his usual occupations on a holiday,
the average man is at a loss for employment. Provided his neighbors are in the same fix, he can play
cards. But there are hobbies and hobbies. As an
occasional relaxation, for example, nothing can be
said against card-playing. But as a hobby it is not
much better than " collecting strings." It is neither
broadening mentally nor invigorating physically, and
it closes the door upon other interests which are both.
I remember that once, on a long sea-voyage, I envied
certain of my fellow-passengers who found amuse-
ment in cards when the conditions were such as to
make almost any other occupation out of the question. But when finally the ship's course lay along a
strange coast, winding among unfamiliar islands,
by shores luxuriant with tropical vegetation and
sprinkled with strange settlements, all affording de-

light to the eye and interest to the mind, these players who had come abroad solely for instruction and pleasure could not be enticed from their tables, and I thanked my stars that I had not fallen under the stultifying sway of cards. Much the same gratitude is aroused when I see men and women spending precious summer days indoors over the card-table when they might be breathing the fragrant, life-giving air, and rejoicing in the beauty and interest of the woods and fields.

All things considered, a hobby that takes us out of doors is the best. The different open-air sports may be classed under this head. The chief lack in the artificial sports, such as polo, golf, baseball, etc., as opposed to the natural sports, hunting and fishing, is that while they are invaluable as a means of health and relaxation, they do not lead to other and broader interests, while many a boy-hunter has developed into a naturalist as a result of long days in the woods. Hunting and fishing would seem almost perfect recreations were it not for the life-taking element, which may become brutalizing. I wish that every mother who believes in the value of natural sport for her young boys would set her face sternly against any taking of life that cannot be justified on the ground of man's needs, either in the way of protection or support.

The ideal hobby, it seems to me, is one that keeps us in the open air among inspiring surroundings, with the knowledge of natural objects as the end in view. The study of plants, of animals, of the earth itself, botany, zoölogy, or geology, any one of these will answer the varied requirements of an ideal hobby. Potentially they possess all the elements of sport. Often they require not only perseverance and skill but courage and daring. They are a means of health, a relaxation to the mind from ordinary cares, and an absorbing interest. Any one of them may be used as a doorway to the others.

If parents realized the value to their childrens' minds and bodies of a love for plants and animals, of any such hobby as birds or butterflies or trees or flowers, I am sure they would take more pains to encourage the interest which instinctively a child feels in these things. It must be because such realization is lacking that we see parents apparently either too indolent or too ignorant to share the enthusiasm and to satisfy the curiosity awakened in the child's active mind by natural objects.

Of course it is possible that owing to the strange reticence of many children, parents may be unconscious of the existence of any enthusiasm or curiosity of this sort. As a little child I was so eager to know the names of the wild flowers that I went through my grandfather's library, examining book after book on flowers in the vain hope of acquiring the desired information. Always after more or less tedious reading, for I was too young to master tables of contents and introductions, I would discover that the volume under examination was devoted to garden flowers. But I do not remember that it occurred to me to tell anyone what I wanted or to ask

3

for help. Finally I learned that a book on the subject, written " for young people," was in existence, and I asked my mother to buy it for me. The request was gratified promptly and I plodded through the preliminary matter of " How Plants Grow " to find that I was quite unable to master the key, and that any knowledge of the flowers that could appeal to my child-mind was locked away from me as hopelessly as before. Even though my one expressed wish had been so gladly met, I did not confide to others my perplexity, but surrendered sadly a cherished dream. Owing largely, I believe, to the reaction from this disappointment, it was many years before I attempted again to wrestle with a botanical key, or to learn the names of the flowers.

How much was lost by yielding too easily to discouragement I not only realize now, but I realized it partially during the long period when the plants were nameless. Among the flowers whose faces were familiar though their names were unknown, I felt that I was not making the most of my opportunities. And when I met plants which were both new and nameless, I was a stranger indeed. In the English woods and along the lovely English rivers, by the rushing torrents and in the Alpine meadows of Switzerland, on the mountains of Brazil, I should have felt myself less an alien had I been able then as now to detect the kinship between foreign and North American plants, and to call the strangers by names that were at least partially familiar.

To the man or woman who is somewhat at home

in the plant-world, travel is quite a different thing from what it is to one who does not know a mint from a mustard. The shortest journey to a new locality is full of interest to the traveller who is striving to lengthen his list of plant acquaintances. The tedious waits around the railway station are welcomed as opportunities for fresh discoveries. The slow local train receives blessings instead of anathemas because of the superiority of its windows as posts of observation. The long stage ride is too short to satisfy the plant-lover who is keeping count of the different species by the roadside.

While crossing the continent on the Canadian Pacific Railway a few years ago, the days spent in traversing the vast plains east of the Rockies were days of keen enjoyment on account of the new plants seen from my window and gathered breathlessly for identification during the brief stops. But to most of my fellow-passengers they were days of unmitigated boredom. They could not comprehend the reluctance with which I met each nightfall as an interruption to my watch.

When, finally, one cold June morning we climbed the glorious Canadian Rockies and were driven to the hotel at Banff, where we were to rest for twenty-four hours, the enjoyment of the previous week was crowned by seeing the dining-room tables decorated with a flower which I had never succeeded in finding in the woods at home. It was the lovely little orchid, *Calypso borealis*, a shy, wild creature which had been brought to me from the mountains of Vermont. It seemed almost desecration to force this little aristocrat to consort with the pepper-pots and pickles of a hotel dining-room. In my eagerness to see Calypso in her forest-home I could scarcely wait to eat the breakfast for which a few moments before I had been painfully hungry.

Unfortunately the waiters at Banff were proved as ruthless as vandals in other parts of the world. Among the pines that clothed the lower mountain-sides I found many plants of Calypso, but only one or two of the delicate blossoms had been left to gladden the eyes of those who love to see a flower in the wild beauty of its natural surroundings.

That same eventful day had in store for me another delight as the result of my love for plants. For a long time I had wished to know the shooting-star, a flower with whose general appearance from pictures or from descriptions I was familiar. I knew that it grew in this part of the world, but during a careful search of the woods and meadows and of the banks of the rushing streams the only shooting-star I discovered was a faded blossom which someone had picked and flung upon the mountain-path. Late in the afternoon, having given up the hope of any fresh find, I went for a swim in the warm sulphur pool. While paddling about the clear water, revelling in the beauty of the surroundings and the sheer physical joy of the moment, my eyes fell suddenly on a cluster of pink, cyclamen-like blossoms springing from the opposite rocks. I recognized at once the pretty shooting-star.

6

Two days later, at Glacier, I had another pleasure from the same source in the discovery of great beds of nodding golden lilies, the western species of adder's tongue, growing close to white fields of snow.

> "Ten thousand saw I at a glance,
> Tossing their heads in sprightly dance."

The enjoyment of the entire trip to the Pacific coast, of the voyage among the islands and glaciers of Alaska, and of the journey home through the Yellowstone and across our Western prairies, was increased indescribably by the new plants I learned to know.

The pleasure we take in literature, as in travel, is enhanced by a knowledge of nature. Not only are we able better to appreciate writers on nature so original and inspiring as Thoreau, or so charming as John Burroughs, but such nature loving poets as Wordsworth, Lowell, Bryant, and countless others, mean infinitely more to the man or woman who with a love of poetry combines a knowledge of the plants and birds mentioned in the poems.

Books of travel are usually far more interesting if we have some knowledge of botany and zoölogy. This is also true of biographies which deal with men or women who find either their work or their recreation—and how many men and women who have been powers for good may be counted in one class or the other—in some department of natural science.

One fascinating department of nature-study, that

of ferns, has received but little attention in this country. Within the last few years we have been supplied with excellent and inexpensive hand-books to our birds, butterflies, trees, and flowers. But so far as I know, with the exception of Mr. Williamson's little volume on the "Ferns of Kentucky," we have no book with sufficient text and illustrations within the reach of the brains and purse of the average fern-lover. In England one finds books of all sizes and prices on the English ferns, while our beautiful American ferns are almost unknown, owing probably to the lack of attractive and inexpensive fern literature. Eaton's finely illustrated work on the "Ferns of North America" is entirely out of the question on account of its expense; and the "Illustrated Flora" of Britton & Brown is also beyond the reach of the ordinary plant-lover. Miss Price's "Fern Collectors' Hand-book" is helpful, but it is without descriptive text. "Our Native Ferns and their Allies," by Mr. Underwood, is exhaustive and authoritative, but it is extremely technical and the different species are not illustrated. Mr. Dodge's pamphlet on the "Ferns and Fern Allies of New England" is excellent so far as it goes, the descriptions not being so technical as to confuse the beginner. But this also is not illustrated, while Mr. Knobel's pamphlet, "The Ferns and Evergreens of New England," has clear black-and-white illustrations of many species, but it has no text of importance.

In view of the singular grace and charm of the fern

tribe, patent to the most careless observer, this lack of fern literature is surprising. It is possible that Thoreau is right in claiming that " we all feel the ferns to be farther from us essentially and sympathetically than the phenogamous plants, the roses and weeds for instance." This may be true in spite of the fact that to some of us the charm of ferns is as great, their beauty more subtle, than that of the flowering plants, and to learn to know them by name, to trace them to their homes, and to observe their habits is attended with an interest as keen, perhaps keener, than that which attends the study of the names, haunts, and habits of the flowers.

That ferns possess a peculiar power of blinding their votaries to the actual position they occupy in the minds of people in general seems to me evidenced by the following quotations, taken respectively from Mr. Underwood's and Mr. Williamson's introductions.

So competent and coldly scientific an authority as Mr. Underwood opens his book with these words :

" In the entire vegetable world there are probably no forms of growth that attract more general notice than the Ferns."

The lack of fern literature, it seems to me, proves the fallacy of this statement. If ferns had been more generally noticed than other " forms of growth " in the vegetable world, surely more would have been written on the subject, and occasionally someone besides a botanist would be found who could

9

name correctly more than three or four of our common wayside ferns.

In his introduction to the "Ferns of Kentucky," Mr. Williamson asks: "Who would now think of going to the country to spend a few days, or even one day, without first inquiring whether ferns are to be found in the locality?"

Though for some years I have been interested in ferns and have made many all-day country expeditions with various friends, I do not remember ever to have heard this question asked. Yet that two such writers as Mr. Underwood and Mr. Williamson could imagine the existence of a state of things so contrary to fact, goes far to prove the fascination of the study.

To the practical mind one of the great advantages of ferns as a hobby lies in the fact that the number of our native, that is, of our northeastern, ferns is so comparatively small as to make it an easy matter to learn to know by name and to see in their homes perhaps two-thirds of them.

On an ordinary walk of an hour or two through the fields and woods, the would-be fern student can familiarize himself with anywhere from ten to fifteen of the ferns described in this book. During a summer holiday in an average locality he should learn to know by sight and by name from twenty-five to thirty ferns, while in a really good neighborhood the enthusiast who is willing to scour the surrounding country from the tops of the highest mountains to the depths of the wildest ravines may hope to extend his list into the forties.

During the past year several lists of the ferns found on a single walk or within a certain radius have been published in the *Fern Bulletin*, leading to some rivalry between fern students who claim precedence for their pet localities.

Mr. Underwood has found twenty-seven species within the immediate vicinity of Green Lake, Onondaga County, N. Y., and thirty-four species within a circle whose diameter is not over three miles.

Mrs. E. H. Terry, on a two-hours' walk near Dorset, Vt., did still better. She found thirty-three species and four varieties, while Miss Margaret Slosson has broken the record by finding thirty-nine species and eight varieties, near Pittsford, Rutland County, Vt., within a triangle formed by "the end of a tamarack swamp, a field less than a mile away, and some limestone cliffs three miles from both the field and the end of the swamp."

Apart from the interest of extending one's list of fern acquaintances is that of discovering new stations for the rarer species. It was my good fortune last summer to make one of a party which found a previously unknown station for the rare Hart's Tongue, and I felt the thrill of excitement which attends such an experience. The other day, in looking over Torrey's "Flora of New York," I noticed the absence of several ferns now known to be natives of this State. When the fern student realizes the possibility which is always before him of finding a new station for a rare fern, and thus adding an item of value to the natural history of the State, he should be stimulated to fresh zeal.

Other interesting possibilities are those of discovering a new variety and of chancing upon those forked or crested fronds which appear occasionally in many species. These unusual forms not only possess the charm of rarity and sometimes of intrinsic beauty, but they are interesting because of the light it is believed they may throw on problems of fern ancestry. To this department of fern study, the discovery and development of abnormal forms, much attention is paid in England. In Lowe's "British Ferns" I find described between thirty and forty varieties of *Polypodium vulgare*, while the varieties of *Scolopendrium vulgare*, our rare Hart's Tongue, extend into the hundreds.

The majority of ferns mature late in the summer, giving the student the advantage of several weeks or months in which to observe their growth. Many of our most interesting flowers bloom and perish before we realize that the spring is really over. There are few flower lovers who have not had the sense of being outwitted by the rush of the season. Every year I make appointments with the different plants to visit them at their flowering time, and nearly every year I miss some such appointments through failure to appreciate the short lives of these fragile blossoms.

A few of the ferns share the early habits common to so many flowers. But usually we can hope to find them in their prime when most of the flowers have disappeared.

To me the greatest charm the ferns possess is that of their surroundings. No other plants know so well how to choose their haunts. If you wish to know the ferns you must follow them to Nature's most sacred retreats. In remote, tangled swamps, overhanging the swift, noiseless brook in the heart of the forest, close to the rush of the foaming water-fall, in the depths of some dark ravine, or perhaps high up on mountain-ledges, where the air is purer and the world wider and life more beautiful than we had fancied, these wild, graceful things are most at home.

You will never learn to know the ferns if you expect to make their acquaintance from a carriage, along the highway, or in the interval between two meals. For their sakes you must renounce indolent habits. You must be willing to tramp tirelessly through woods and across fields, to climb mountains and to scramble down gorges. You must be content with what luncheon you can carry in your pocket. And let me tell you this. When at last you fling yourself upon some bed of springing moss, and add to your sandwich cresses fresh and dripping from the neighboring brook, you will eat your simple meal with a relish that never attends the most elaborate luncheon within four walls. And when later you surrender yourself to the delicious sense of fatigue and drowsy relaxation which steals over you, mind and body, listening half-unconsciously to the plaintive, long-drawn notes of the wood-birds and the sharp "tsing" of the locusts, breathing the mingled fragrance of the mint at your feet and the pines and hemlocks overhead, you will wonder vaguely why on summer days you ever drive along the dusty high-road or eat indoors or do any of the flavorless conventional things that consume so large a portion of our lives.

Of course what is true of other out-door studies is true of the study of ferns. Constantly your curiosity is aroused by some bird-note, some tree, some gorgeously colored butterfly, and, in the case of ferns especially, by some outcropping rock, which make you eager to follow up other branches of nature-study, and to know by name each tree and bird and butterfly and rock you meet.

The immediate result of these long happy days is that "golden doze of mind which follows upon much exercise in the open air," the "ecstatic stupor" which Stevenson supposes to be the nearly chronic condition of "open-air laborers." Surely there is no such preventive of insomnia, no such cure for nervousness or morbid introspection as an absorbing out-door interest. Body and mind alike are invigorated to a degree that cannot be appreciated by one who has not experienced the life-giving power of some such close and loving contact with nature.

WHEN AND WHERE TO FIND FERNS

IT is in early spring that one likes to take up for the first time an out-door study. But if you begin your search for ferns in March, when the woods are yielding a few timid blossoms, and the air, still pungent with a suggestion of winter, vibrates to the lisping notes of newly arrived birds, you will hardly be rewarded by finding any but the evergreen species, and even these are not likely to be especially conspicuous at this season.

Usually it is the latter part of April before the pioneers among the ferns, the great Osmundas, push up the big, woolly croziers, or fiddleheads, which will soon develop into the most luxuriant and tropical-looking plants of our low wet woods and roadsides.

At about the same time, down among last year's Christmas Ferns, you find the rolled-up fronds of this year, covered with brown or whitish scales. And now every day for many weeks will appear fresh batches of young ferns. Someone has said that there is nothing more aggressively new-born than a young fern, and this thought will recur constantly as you chance upon the little wrinkled crozier-like fronds, whether they are bundled up in wrappings of soft wool or protected by a garment of overlapping scales, or whether, like many of the later arrivals, they come into the world as naked and puny as a human baby.

Once uncurled, the ferns lose quickly this look of infancy, and embody, quite as effectively, even the hardiest and coarsest among them, the slender grace of youth. Early in May we find the Osmundas in this stage of their development. The Royal Fern, smooth and delicate, is now flushing the wet meadows with its tender red. In the open woods and along the roadside the Interrupted and the Cinnamon Ferns wear a green equally delicate. These three plants soon reach maturity and are conspicuous by reason of their unusual size and their flower-like fruit-clusters.

On the rocky banks of the brook, or perhaps among the spreading roots of some forest-tree, the Fragile Bladder Fern unrolls its tremulous little

Fiddleheads

18

fronds, on which the fruit-dots soon appear. Where there is less moisture and more exposure we may find the Rusty Woodsia, now belying its name by its silvery aspect. At this same season in the bogs and thickets we should look for the curious little Adder's Tongue.

By the first of June many of the ferns are well advanced. On the hill-sides and along the wood-path the Brake spreads its single umbrella-like frond, now pale green and delicate, quite unlike the umbrageous-looking plant of a month later. Withdrawing into the recesses formed by the pasture-rails the Lady Fern is in its first freshness, without any sign of the disfigurements it develops so often by the close of the summer. Great patches of yellowish green in the wet meadows draw attention to the Sensitive Fern, which only at this season seems to have any claim to its

Fragile Bladder Fern

title. The Virginia Chain Fern is another plant to be looked for in the wet June meadows. It is one of the few ferns which grows occasionally in deep water.

The Maidenhair, though immature, is lovely in its fragility. Thoreau met with it on June 13th and describes it in his diary for that day: "The delicate maiden-hair fern forms a cup or dish, very delicate and graceful. Beautiful, too, its glossy black stem and its wave-edged, fruited leaflets."

In the crevices of lofty cliffs the Mountain Spleenwort approaches maturity. And now we should search the moist, mossy crannies of the rocks for the Slender Cliff Brake, for in some localities this plant disappears early in the summer.

We may hope to find most of the ferns in full foliage, if not in fruit, by the middle of July. Dark green, tall and vigorous stand the Brakes. The Crested Shield Fern is fruiting in the swamps, and in the deeper woods Clinton's and Goldie's Ferns are in full fruitage. Magnificent vase-like clusters of the Ostrich Fern spread above our

Crested
Shield Fern

heads in the thicket along the river-shore. The Spinulose Shield Fern and the Evergreen Wood Fern meet us at every turn of the shaded path beside the brook, and on the rocky wooded hillside the Christmas Fern is almost as abundant. Where the stream plunges from above, the Bulblet Bladder Fern drapes the steep banks with its long feathery fronds. In the wet meadows and thickets the New York Fern and the Marsh Shield Fern are noticeable on account of their light green color and delicate texture. On mountain-ledges we look for the little Woodsias, and in rocky places, often in the shadow of red cedars, for the slim erect fronds of the Ebony Spleenwort.

Possibly it will be our good fortune to discover the blue-green foliage of the Purple Cliff Brake springing from the crevices of some dry limestone cliff. Almost surely, if we search the moist, shaded rocks and ravines in the neighborhood, we shall greet with unfailing pleasure the lovely little Maidenhair Spleenwort.

In somewhat southern localities the tapering, yellow-green fronds of the *Dicksonia* or Hay-scented Fern are even more abundant and conspicuous than the darker foliage of the Spinulose Shield Fern. They abound along the roadsides and in partially shaded or open pastures, the spores ripening not earlier than August.

In the same month we find in full maturity three interesting wood ferns, all belonging to the same group. The first of these is the Long Beech Fern.

It is abundant in many of our northern woods **and** on the rocky banks of streams. Its shape is noticeably triangular, the triangle being longer than broad. Its texture is rather soft and downy. The lowest pair of pinnæ stand forward and are conspicuously deflexed, giving an easy clew to the plant's identity.

The most attractive member of the group to my mind is the Oak Fern. I find it growing abundantly in the cedar swamps and wet woods of somewhat northern localities. Its delicate, spreading, three-branched frond suggests that of a young Brake. This plant is peculiarly dainty in the early summer, as frequently later in the year it becomes blotched and disfigured.

Purple Cliff Brake

The Broad Beech Fern seeks drier neighborhoods, and often a more southern locality than its two kinsmen. Its triangular fronds, broader than they are long, are conspicuous on account of the unusual size of the lowest pair of pinnæ.

A common plant in the rich August woods is the Virginia Grape Fern, with its spreading leaf and branching fruit-cluster. The rather coarsely cut fronds of the Silvery Spleenwort are also frequently met with in the same neighborhood. Occasionally in their companionship we find the delicate and attractive Narrow-leaved Spleenwort.

August is the month that should be chosen for expeditions in search of some of our rarest ferns. In certain wild ravines of Central New York, at the foot of shaded limestone cliffs, the glossy leaves of the Hart's Tongue are actually weighed down by the brown, velvety rows of sporangia which emboss their lower surfaces. Over the rocks near-by, the quaint, though less unusual, Walking Leaf runs riot. Perhaps in the crevices of the overhanging cliff the little Rue Spleenwort has secured a foothold for its tiny fronds, their backs nearly covered with confluent fruit-dots.

On the mountain-ledges of Northern New England we should look for the Green Spleenwort, and for the Fragrant Shield Fern. Along rocky mountain-streams Braun's Holly Fern may be found. In wet woods, usually near the coast, the Net-veined Chain Fern is occasionally conspicuous.

More southern localities must be visited if we wish to see in its home the Hairy Lip Fern, whose most northern stations were on the Hudson River (for I do not know if this plant can be found there at

23

present), and such rare Spleenworts as the Pinnatifid, Scott's and Bradley's.

In September the fruit-clusters of the little Curly Grass ripen in the low pine barrens of New Jersey. Over moist thickets, in rarely favored retreats from Massachusetts southward, clamber the slender strands of the Climbing Fern. Thoreau's diary of September 26th evidently refers to this plant: "The tree-fern is in

Ternate Grape Fern

24

fruit now, with its delicate, tendril-like fruit, climbing three or four feet over the asters, golden-rod, etc., on the edge of the swamp."

In moist places now we find the triangular much dissected leaf and branching fruit-cluster of the Ternate Grape Fern.

When October sets in, many of the ferns take their color-note from the surroundings. Vying with the maples along the roadside the Osmundas wear deep orange. Many of the fronds of the *Dicksonia* are bleached almost white, while others look fresh and green despite their delicate texture. On October 4th Thoreau writes of this plant:

"How interesting now, by wall-sides and on open springy hill-sides, the large straggling tufts of the Dicksonia fern above the leaf-strewn green sward, the cold, fall-green sward! They are unusually preserved about the Corner Spring, considering the earliness of this year. Long, handsome, lanceolate green fronds pointing in every direction, recurved and full of fruit, intermixed with yellowish and sere brown and shrivelled ones, the whole clump perchance strewn with fallen and withered maple leaves, and overtopped by now withered and unnoticed osmundas. Their lingering greenness is so much the more noticeable now that the leaves generally have changed. They affect us as if they were evergreen, such persistent life and greenness in the midst of decay. No matter how much they are strewn with withered leaves, moist and green they spire above them, not fearing the frosts, fragile as they are.

25

Their greenness is so much the more interesting, because so many have already fallen, and we know that the first severe frost will cut off them too. In the summer greenness is cheap, now it is a thing comparatively rare, and is the emblem of life to us."

Oddly enough, with the first approach of winter the vigorous-looking Brake turns brown and quickly withers, usually without passing through any intermediate gradations of yellow.

In November we notice chiefly the evergreen ferns. The great round fruit-dots of the Polypody show distinctly through the fronds as they stand erect in the sunlight. A sober green, looking as though it were warranted fast, is the winter dress of the Evergreen Wood Fern. The Christmas Fern, bright and glossy, reminds one that the holiday season is not distant. These three plants are especially conspicuous in our late autumn woods. Their brave and cheerful endurance is always a delight. Later in the season the curled pinnæ of the Polypody seem to be making the best of cold weather. The fronds of the Christmas Fern and the Evergreen Wood Fern, still fresh and green, lie prostrate on the ground, their weakened stems apparently unable to support them erect, but undoubtedly in this position they are the better protected from the storm and stress of winter.

Many other ferns are more or less evergreen, but perhaps none are so important to our fall rambles as this sturdy group. Several of the Rock Spleenworts are evergreen, but their ordinarily diminutive stature dwindles with the increasing cold, and we seldom encounter them on our winter walks. The sterile fronds of a number of the Shield Ferns endure till spring. The Purple Cliff Brake and the Walking Leaf are also proof against ice and snow. Even in the middle of January the keen-eyed fern hunter may hope to make some discovery of interest regarding the haunts and habits of his favorites.

Evergreen Wood Fern

EXPLANATION OF TERMS

A FERN is a flowerless plant growing from a *rootstock* (*a*), with leaves or *fronds* usually raised on a stalk, rolled up (*b*) in the bud,* and bearing on their lower surfaces (*c*) the *spores*, by means of which the plant reproduces.

A *rootstock* is an underground, rooting stem. Ferns are propagated by the growth and budding of the rootstock as well as by the ordinary method of reproduction. The fronds spring from the rootstock in the manner peculiar to the species to which they belong. The Osmundas, the Evergreen Wood Fern, and others grow in a crown or circle, the younger fronds always inside. The Mountain Spleenwort is one of a class which has irregularly clus-

* *Ophioglossum* and the Botrychiums, not being true ferns, are exceptions.

Polypody

28

tered fronds. The fronds of the Brake are more or less solitary, rising from distinct and somewhat distant portions of the rootstock. The Botrychiums usually give birth to a single frond each season, the base of the stalk containing the bud for the succeeding year.

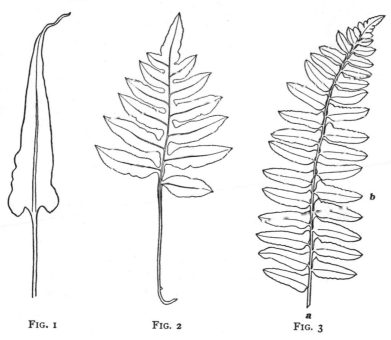

FIG. 1   FIG. 2   FIG. 3

A frond is *simple* when it consists of an undivided leaf such as that of the Hart's Tongue or of the Walking Leaf (Fig. 1).

A frond is *pinnatifid* when cut so as to form lobes extending half-way or more to the midvein (Fig. 2).

A frond is *once-pinnate* when the incisions extend to the midvein (Fig. 3). Under these conditions the midvein is called the *rachis* (*a*), and the divisions are called the *pinnæ* (*b*).

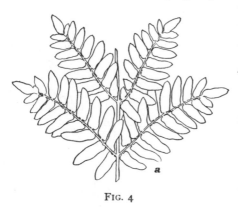

FIG. 4

A frond is *twice-pinnate* when the pinnæ are cut into divisions which extend to their midveins (Fig. 4). These divisions of the pinnæ are called *pinnules* (*a*).

A frond that is only once-pinnate may seem at first glance twice-pinnate, as its pinnæ may be so deeply lobed or pinnatifid as to require a close examination to convince us that the lobes come short of the midvein of the pinnæ. In a popular hand-book it is not thought necessary to explain further modifications.

FIG. 5

The veins of a fern are *free* when, branching from the midvein, they do not unite with other veins (Fig. 5).

FIG. 6

Ferns produce *spores* (Fig. 6) instead of seeds. These spores are collected in spore-cases or *sporangia* (Fig. 7). Usually the sporangia are clustered in dots or lines on the back of a frond or along its margins. These patches of sporangia are called *sori* or *fruit-*

dots. They take various shapes in the different species. They may be round or linear or oblong or kidney-shaped or curved. At times they are naked, but more frequently they are covered by a minute outgrowth of the frond or by its reflexed margin. This covering is called the *indusium.* In systematic botanies the indusia play an important part in determining genera. But as often they are so minute as to be almost invisible to the naked eye, and, as frequently they wither away early in the season, I place little dependence upon them as a means of popular identification.

FIG. 7

A *fertile* frond is one which bears spores.

A *sterile* frond is one without spores.

31

FERTILIZATION, DEVELOPMENT, AND FRUCTIFICATION OF FERNS

UNTIL very recently the development of ferns, their methods of fertilization and fructification have been shrouded in mystery. At one period it was believed that "fern-seed," as the fern-spores were called, possessed various miraculous powers. These were touched upon frequently by the early poets. In Shakespeare's " Henry IV " Gadshill exclaims:

"We have the receipt of fern-seed, we walk invisible."

He is met with the rejoinder:

" Nay, I think rather you are more beholden to the night than to fern-seed, for your walking invisible."

One of Ben Jonson's characters expresses the same idea in much the same words:

"I had no medicine, sir, to walk invisible,
No fern-seed in my pocket."

In Butler's "Hudibras" reference is made to the anxieties we needlessly create for ourselves:

" That spring like fern, that infant weed,
Equivocally without seed,
And have no possible foundation
But merely in th' imagination."

In view of the fact that many ferns bear their spores or "fern-seed" somewhat conspicuously on the lower surfaces of their fronds, it seems probable that the "fern" of early writers was our common Brake, the fructification of which is more than usually obscure, its sporangia or "fern-seed" being concealed till full maturity by the reflexed margin of its frond. This plant is, perhaps, the most abundant and conspicuous of English ferns. Miss Pratt believes it to be the "fearn" of the Anglo-Saxons, and says that to its profusion in their neighborhood many towns and hamlets, such as Fearnborough or Farnborough, Farningham, Farnhow, and others owe their titles. The plant is a noticeable and common one also on the Continent.

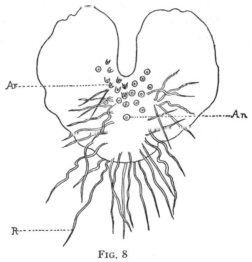

FIG. 8

In 1848 the development of the fern was first satisfactorily explained. It was then shown that these plants pass through what has been called, not altogether happily the modern botanist thinks, an "alternation of generations." One "generation," the "sexual," consists of a tiny, green, plate-like object, termed the

33

prothallium (Fig. 8). This is connected with the soil by hair-like roots. On its lower surface are borne usually both the reproductive organs of the fern, the *antheridia*, corresponding to the stamens or fertilizing organs of the flower, and the *archegonia*, performing the office of the flower's pistils, inasmuch as their germ-cells receive the fertilizing substance produced by the *antheridia*. But no seeds are formed as the result of this fertilization. Instead of this seed-formation which we note in the flowering plant, the germ-cell in the fern develops into a fern-plant, which forms the "asexual" generation.

The first fronds of this little plant are very small and simple, quite unlike the later ones. For a time the plant is nourished by the prothallium, but as soon as it is sufficiently developed and vigorous enough to shift for itself, the prothallium dies away, and the fern maintains an independent existence.

FIG. 9   FIG. 10   FIG. 11
First fronds of Maidenhair

Eventually it produces fronds which bear on their lower surfaces the sporangia containing the minute spores from which spring the prothallia.

For our present purpose it is enough to say that spores differ from seeds in that they are not the immediate result of the interaction of reproductive organs. They resemble seeds in that they are expelled from the parent-plant on attaining maturity, and germinate on contact with the moist earth.

Thus it is seen that the life-cycle of a fern consists of two stages:

First, the prothallium, bearing the reproductive organs; second, the fern-plant proper, developing the spores which produce the prothallium.

Along the moist, shaded banks of the wood road, or on decaying stumps, keen eyes will discern frequently the tiny green prothallia, although they are somewhat difficult to find except in the green-house where one can see them in abundance either in the boxes used for growing the young plants, or on the moist surfaces of flower-pots, where the spores have fallen accidentally and have germinated.

As the fertilization of the germ-cell in the archegonium cannot take place except under water, perhaps the fact is accounted for that ferns are found chiefly in moist places. This water may be only a sufficient amount of rain or dew to permit the antherozoids or fertilizing cells of the antheridium to swim to the archegonium, which they enter for the purpose of fertilizing the germ-cell.

It is interesting to examine with a good magnifying glass the sporangia borne on the lower surface of a mature fertile frond. In many species each sporangium or spore-case is surrounded with an elastic ring, which at maturity contracts so suddenly as to rupture the spore-case, and cause the expulsion of the numberless spores (Fig. 7).

NOTABLE FERN FAMILIES

OSMUNDA (Flowering Ferns)

Tall swamp ferns, growing in large crowns, with the fertile fronds or portions *conspicuously unlike* the sterile ; sporangia opening by a longitudinal cleft into two valves.

ONOCLEA

Coarse ferns, with the fertile fronds rolled up into necklace-like or berry-like segments, and *entirely unlike* the broad, pinnatifid sterile ones. Fertile fronds unrolling at maturity, allowing the spores to escape, and remaining long after the sterile fronds have perished ; sporangia stalked, ringed, bursting transversely.

WOODSIA

Small or medium-sized ferns, growing among rocks, with 1-2 pinnate or pinnatifid fronds and round fruit-dots ; indusium thin and often evanescent, attached by its base under the sporangia, either small and open, or else early bursting at the top into irregular pieces or lobes ; sporangia stalked, ringed, bursting transversely.

CYSTOPTERIS (Bladder Ferns)

Delicate rock or wood ferns, with 2-3 pinnate fronds and round fruit-dots ; indusium hood-like, attached by a broad base to the inner side, soon thrown back or withering away ; sporangia as above.

ASPIDIUM (Shield Ferns)

Ferns with 1-3 pinnate fronds and round fruit-dots ; indusium more or less flat, fixed by its depressed centre ; sporangia as above.

PHEGOPTERIS (Beech Ferns)

Medium-sized or small ferns, with 2–3 pinnatifid or ternate leaves, and small, round, uncovered fruit-dots; sporangia as above.

WOODWARDIA (Chain Ferns)

Large and rather coarse ferns of swamps or wet woods, fronds pinnate or nearly twice-pinnate; fruit-dots oblong or linear, sunk in cavities of the leaf and arranged in chain-like rows; indusium lid-like, somewhat leathery, fixed by its outer margin to a veinlet; veins more or less reticulated; sporangia as above.

ASPLENIUM (Spleenworts)

Large or small ferns, with varying fronds and linear or oblong fruit-dots; indusium straight or curved; sporangia as above.

PELLÆA (Cliff Brakes)

Small or medium-sized rock ferns, with pinnate fronds and sporangia borne beneath the reflexed margins of the pinnæ; sporangia as above.

BOTRYCHIUM (Moonworts)

(Belonging to the Fern Allies)

Fleshy plants, with fronds (usually solitary) divided into a sterile and a fertile portion, the bud for the succeeding year embedded in the base of the stem.

HOW TO USE THE BOOK

BEFORE attempting to identify the ferns by means of the following Guide it would be well to turn to the Explanation of Terms, and with as many species as you can conveniently collect, on the table before you, to master the few necessary technical terms, that you may be able to distinguish a frond that is pinnatifid from one that is pinnate, a pinna from a pinnule, a fertile from a sterile frond.

You should bear in mind that in some species the fertile fronds are so unleaf-like in appearance that to the uninitiated they do not suggest fronds at all. The fertile fronds of the Onocleas, for example, are so contracted as to conceal any resemblance to the sterile ones. They appear to be mere clusters of fruit. The fertile fronds of the Cinnamon Fern are equally unleaf-like, as are the fertile portions of the other Osmundas and of several other species.

In your rambles through the fields and woods your eyes will soon learn to detect hitherto unnoticed species. In gathering specimens you will take heed to break off the fern as near the ground as possible, and you will not be satisfied till you have secured both a fertile and a sterile frond. In carrying them home you will remember the necessity of keeping together the fronds which belong to the same plant.

When sorting your finds you will group them according to the Guide. The broad-leaved Sensitive Fern, with its separate, dark-green fruit cluster, makes its way necessarily to Group I. To Group II goes your pale-fronded Royal Fern, tipped with brown sporangia. As a matter of course you lay in Group III the leaf-like but dissimilar sterile and fertile fronds of the Slender Cliff Brake. The spreading Brake, its reflexed margin covering the sporangia, identifies itself with Group IV. The oblong fruit-dots of the little Mountain Spleenwort carry it to Group V, while the round ones, like pinheads, of the Evergreen Wood Fern announce it a member of Group VI.

The different ferns sorted, it will be a simple matter to run quickly through the brief descriptions under the different Groups till you are referred to the descriptions in the body of the book of the species under investigation.

GUIDE

FOR the purpose of identification the ferns described are arranged in six groups, according to their manner of fruiting.

GROUP I

STERILE AND FERTILE FRONDS TOTALLY UNLIKE; FERTILE FRONDS NOT LEAF-LIKE IN APPEARANCE

1. SENSITIVE FERN

Onoclea sensibilis

Sterile fronds usually large; broadly triangular, deeply pinnatifid. Fertile fronds much contracted, with berry-like pinnules. In wet meadows. P. 54.

2. OSTRICH FERN

Onoclea Struthiopteris

Large. Sterile fronds once-pinnate, pinnæ pinnatifid. Fertile fronds contracted, with necklace-like pinnæ. Along streams and in moist woods. P. 56.

3. CINNAMON FERN

Osmunda cinnamomea

Large. Sterile fronds once-pinnate, pinnæ pinnatifid. Fertile fronds composed of cinnamon-brown fruit-clusters. In wet places. P. 60.

4. CURLY GRASS

Schizæa pusilla

Very small. Sterile fronds linear, grass-like. Fertile fronds taller, with a terminal fruit-cluster. In pine barrens of New Jersey. P. 63.

GROUP II

FERTILE FRONDS PARTIALLY LEAF-LIKE, THE FERTILE PORTION UNLIKE THE REST OF THE FROND

[The species coming under the genera *Botrychium* and *Ophioglossum* may appear to belong to Group I, as the fertile and the sterile portions of their fronds may seem to the uninitiated like separate fronds, but in reality they belong to the one frond.]

5. ROYAL FERN

Osmunda regalis

Large. Sterile fronds twice-pinnate, pinnules oblong. Fertile fronds leaf-like below, sporangia in clusters at their summits. In wet places. P. 67.

6. INTERRUPTED FERN

Osmunda Claytoniana

Large. Sterile fronds once-pinnate, pinnæ pinnatifid. Fertile fronds leaf-like above and below, contracted in the middle with brown fruit-clusters. In wet places. P. 72.

7. CLIMBING FERN

Lygodium palmatum

Climbing, with lobed, palmate pinnæ and terminal fruit-clusters. Moist thickets and open woods. Rare. P. 75.

8. ADDER'S TONGUE

Ophioglossum vulgatum

Small. Sterile portion an ovate leaf. Fertile portion a slender spike. In moist meadows. P. 77.

9. RATTLESNAKE FERN

Botrychium Virginianum

Rather large. Sterile portion a thin, spreading, ternately divided leaf with three primary divisions ; 1–2 pinnate. Fertile portion a branching fruit-cluster. In rich woods. P. 80.

41

10. TERNATE GRAPE FERN

Botrychium ternatum or *dissectum*

Of varying size, very fleshy. Sterile portion a broadly triangular, ternate, finely dissected leaf, long-stalked from near the base of the stem. Fertile portion a branching fruit-cluster. In moist meadows. P. 81.

11. LITTLE GRAPE FERN

Botrychium simplex

A very small fleshy plant. Sterile portion an oblong leaf more or less lobed. Fertile portion a simple or slightly branching spike. In moist woods and in fields. P. 82.

12. MOONWORT

Botrychium Lunaria

Usually small, very fleshy. Sterile portion divided into several fan-shaped lobes. Fertile portion a branching fruit-cluster. Mostly in fields. P. 84.

13. MATRICARY GRAPE FERN

Botrychium matricariæfolium

Small, more or less fleshy. Sterile portion ovate or oblong, once or twice pinnatifid. Fertile portion a branching fruit-cluster. In grassy woods and wet meadows. P. 86.

14. LANCE-LEAVED GRAPE FERN

Botrychium lanceolatum

Small, scarcely fleshy. Sterile portion triangular, twice-pinnatifid. Fertile portion a branching fruit-cluster. In woods and meadows. P. 86.

GROUP III

FERTILE FRONDS UNIFORMLY SOMEWHAT LEAF-LIKE IN APPEARANCE, YET DIFFERING NOTICEABLY FROM STERILE FRONDS

15. SLENDER CLIFF BRAKE

Pellæa gracilis

A small fern, 1–3 pinnate. Very delicate. Fertile fronds taller, more contracted and simpler than the sterile, sporangia bordering the pinnæ. Usually on sheltered rocks, preferring limestone. P. 87.

16. PURPLE CLIFF BRAKE

Pellæa atropurpurea

Medium sized, 1–2 pinnate, leathery. Fertile fronds taller and more contracted than the sterile, sporangia bordering the pinnæ. Usually on exposed rocks, preferring limestone. P. 90.

17. CHRISTMAS FERN

Aspidium acrostichoides

Rather large, smooth and glossy, once-pinnate. Fertile fronds contracted at the summit where the fruit appears. In rocky woods. P. 96.

18. NARROW-LEAVED SPLEENWORT

Asplenium angustifolium

Tall and delicate, once-pinnate. Fertile fronds taller and narrower than the sterile. In moist woods in late summer. P.98.

19. NET-VEINED CHAIN FERN

Woodwardia angustifolia

Large, fronds deeply pinnatifid, the fertile taller and more contracted than the sterile. In wet woods near the coast. P. 102.

GROUP IV

FERTILE AND STERILE FRONDS LEAF-LIKE AND SIMILAR; SPORANGIA ON OR BENEATH A REFLEXED PORTION OF THE MARGIN

[The first clause bars out *P. gracilis* and *P. atropurpurea*, which otherwise would belong to Group IV as well as to Group III.]

20. BRAKE

Pteris aquilina

Large and coarse, frond 3-branched, spreading, each branch 2-pinnate, sporangia in a continuous line beneath the reflexed margin of the frond. In dry, somewhat open places. P. 105.

21. MAIDENHAIR

Adiantum pedatum

Graceful and delicate, frond forked at the summit of the stem, 2-pinnate, the pinnæ springing from the upper sides of the branches, pinnules one-sided, their upper margins lobed, bearing on their undersides the short fruit-dots. In rich woods. P. 108.

22. HAIRY LIP FERN

Cheilanthes vestita

Rather small, fronds 2-pinnate, hairy, fruit-dots "covered by the infolded ends of the rounded or oblong lobes." On rocks. P. 112.

23. HAY-SCENTED FERN

Dicksonia pilosiuscula

Rather large, pale, delicate and sweet-scented, fronds usually 2-pinnate, fruit-dots small, each on a recurved toothlet of the pinnule, borne on an elevated, globular receptacle. In moist thickets and in upland pastures. P. 114.

GROUP V

FERTILE AND STERILE FRONDS LEAF-LIKE AND SIMILAR; SPORANGIA IN LINEAR OR OBLONG FRUIT-DOTS

24. LADY FERN

Asplenium Filix-fœmina

Rather large, fronds 2-pinnate, fruit-dots curved, often horse-shoe shaped, finally confluent. In moist woods and along road-sides. P. 120.

25. SILVERY SPLEENWORT

Asplenium thelypteroides

Large, fronds once-pinnate, pinnæ deeply pinnatifid, lobes ob-long and obtuse, fruit-dots oblong, silvery when young. In rich woods. P. 124.

26. RUE SPLEENWORT

Asplenium Ruta-muraria

Very small, fronds loosely 2–3 pinnate at base, pinnatifid above, fruit-dots linear-oblong, confluent when mature. On limestone cliffs. Rare. P. 126.

27. MOUNTAIN SPLEENWORT

Asplenium montanum

Small, fronds 1–2 pinnate, fruit-dots linear-oblong, often conflu-ent. On rocks. P. 130.

28. EBONY SPLEENWORT

Asplenium ebeneum

Fronds slender and erect, once-pinnate, pinnæ eared on the up-per or on both sides, stalk and rachis blackish and shining, fruit-dots oblong. On rocks and hill-sides. P. 134.

29. MAIDENHAIR SPLEENWORT

Asplenium Trichomanes

Small, fronds once-pinnate, pinnæ roundish, stalk and rachis purplish-brown and shining, fruit-dots short. In crevices of rocks. P. 136.

30. GREEN SPLEENWORT

Asplenium viride

Small, fronds linear, once-pinnate, brownish stalk passing into a green rachis. On shaded cliffs northward. P. 138.

31. SCOTT'S SPLEENWORT

Asplenium ebenoides

Small, fronds pinnate below, pinnatifid above, apex slender and prolonged, stalk and rachis blackish, fruit-dots straight or slightly curved. On limestone. Very rare. P. 140.

32. PINNATIFID SPLEENWORT

Asplenium pinnatifidum

Small, fronds pinnatifid, or the lower part pinnate, tapering above into a slender prolongation, stalk blackish, passing into a green rachis, fruit-dots straight or slightly curved. On rocks. Rare. P. 142.

33. BRADLEY'S SPLEENWORT

Asplenium Bradleyi

Small, once-pinnate, pinnæ lobed or toothed, stalk and rachis chestnut-brown, fruit-dots short. On rocks, preferring limestone. Very rare. P. 144.

34. WALKING FERN

Camptosorus rhizophyllus

Small, fronds undivided, heart-shaped at the base or sometimes with prolonged basal ears, tapering above to a prolonged point which roots, forming a new plant, fruit-dots oblong or linear, irregularly scattered. On shaded rocks, preferring limestone. P. 146.

35. HART'S TONGUE

Scolopendrium vulgare

Fronds a few inches to nearly two feet long, undivided, oblong-lanceolate, heart-shaped at base, fruit-dots linear, elongated. Growing among the fragments of limestone cliffs. Very rare. P. 150.

36. VIRGINIA CHAIN FERN

Woodwardia Virginica

Large, fronds once-pinnate, pinnæ pinnatifid, fruit-dots oblong, in chain-like rows parallel and near to the midrib, confluent when ripe. In swamps. P. 156.

GROUP VI

FERTILE AND STERILE FRONDS LEAF-LIKE AND USUALLY
SIMILAR, FRUIT-DOTS ROUND

37. NEW YORK FERN

Aspidium Noveboracense

Usually rather tall, fronds once-pinnate, with deeply pinnatifid pinnæ, tapering both ways from the middle, margins of fertile fronds not revolute. In woods and open meadows. P. 159.

38. MARSH FERN

Aspidium Thelypteris

Usually rather tall, fronds once-pinnate, with pinnæ deeply pinnatifid, scarcely narrower at the base than at the middle, veins forked, fertile fronds noticeable from their *strongly revolute* margins. In wet woods and open swamps. P. 160.

39. MASSACHUSETTS FERN

Aspidium simulatum

Close to preceding species, rather tall, fronds once-pinnate, with pinnatifid pinnæ little or not at all narrowed at base, veins not forked, margin of fertile frond slightly revolute. In wooded swamps. P. 164.

CHRISTMAS FERN

Aspidium acrostichoides

[See No. 17]

40. SPINULOSE WOOD FERN

Aspidium spinulosum var. intermedium

Very common, usually but not always large, fronds oblong-ovate, 2–3 pinnate, lowest pinnæ unequally triangular-ovate, lobes of pinnæ thorny-toothed.   In woods everywhere.   P. 166.

41. BOOTT'S SHIELD FERN

Aspidium Boottii

From one and a half to more than three feet high.   Sterile fronds smaller and simpler than the fertile, nearly or quite twice-pinnate, the lowest pinnæ triangular-ovate, upper longer and narrower, pinnules oblong-ovate, sharply thorny-toothed.   In moist woods. P. 168.

42. CRESTED SHIELD FERN

Aspidium cristatum

Usually rather large, fronds linear-oblong or lanceolate, once pinnate with pinnatifid pinnæ, linear-oblong, fruit-dots between midvein and margin.   In swamps.   P. 170.

43. CLINTON'S WOOD FERN

Aspidium cristatum, var. Clintonianum

In every way larger than preceding species, fronds usually twice-pinnate, pinnæ *broadest at base*, fruit-dots near the midvein.   In swampy woods.   P. 172.

44. GOLDIE'S FERN

Aspidium Goldianum

Large, fronds broadly ovate or the fertile ovate-oblong, once-pinnate with pinnatifid pinnæ, pinnæ *broadest in the middle*, fruit-dots very near the midvein.   In rich woods.   P. 175.

45. EVERGREEN WOOD FERN

Aspidium marginale

Very common, usually rather large, smooth, somewhat leathery, fronds ovate oblong, 1–2 pinnate, fruit-dots large, distinct, close to the margin. In rocky woods. P. 176.

46. FRAGRANT SHIELD FERN

Aspidium fragrans

Small, fragrant, fronds once-pinnate, with pinnatifid pinnæ, stalk and rachis chaffy, fruit-dots large. On rocks northward, especially near waterfalls. P. 178.

47. BRAUN'S HOLLY FERN

Aspidium aculeatum var. Braunii

Rather large, fronds oblong-lanceolate, twice-pinnate, pinnules sharply toothed, covered with long, soft hairs, fruit-dots small. In deep, rocky woods. P. 182.

48. COMMON POLYPODY

Polypodium vulgare

Usually small, fronds somewhat leathery, narrowly oblong, fruit-dots large, round, uncovered, half-way between midvein and margin. On rocks. P. 184.

HAY-SCENTED FERN

Dicksonia pilosiuscula

[See No. 23]

49. LONG BEECH FERN

Phegopteris polypodioides

Medium-sized, fronds downy, triangular, longer than broad, once-pinnate, pinnæ pinnatifid ; lowest pair deflexed and standing forward. In moist woods and on the banks of streams. P. 187.

50. BROAD BEECH FERN

Phegopteris hexagonoptera

Larger than the preceding species, fronds triangular, as broad or broader than long, once-pinnate, pinnæ pinnatifid, lowest pair very large, basal segments of pinnæ forming a continuous, many-angled wing along the rachis. In dry woods and on hill-sides. P. 188.

51. OAK FERN

Phegopteris Dryopteris

Medium-sized, fronds thin and delicate, broadly triangular, spreading, ternate, the three divisions stalked, each division pinnate, pinnæ pinnatifid. In moist woods. P. 190.

52. BULBLET BLADDER FERN

Cystopteris bulbifera

Fronds delicate, elongated, tapering above from a broad base, 2-3 pinnate or pinnatifid, bearing fleshy bulblets beneath. On wet rocks, preferring limestone. P. 194.

53. COMMON BLADDER FERN

Cystopteris fragilis

Medium-sized, fronds thin, oblong-lanceolate, 2–3 pinnate or pinnatifid. On rocks and in moist woods. P. 198.

54. RUSTY WOODSIA

Woodsia Ilvensis

Small, more or less covered with rusty hairs, fronds lanceolate, once-pinnate, pinnæ pinnatifid. On exposed rocks. P. 200.

55. BLUNT-LOBED WOODSIA

Woodsia obtusa

Small, slightly downy, fronds broadly lanceolate, nearly twice-pinnate. On rocks. P. 202.

56. NORTHERN WOODSIA

Woodsia hyperborea

Very small, smooth or nearly so, fronds narrowly oblong-lanceo-late, once-pinnate, pinnæ cordate-ovate or triangular-ovate, 5–7 lobed. On moist rocks. P. 203.

57. SMOOTH WOODSIA

Woodsia glabella

Very small, smooth throughout and delicate, fronds linear, once-pinnate, pinnæ roundish ovate, lobed. On moist rocks. P. 206.

FERN DESCRIPTIONS

"Nature made a fern for pure leaves."—*Thoreau*

GROUP I

STERILE AND FERTILE FRONDS TOTALLY UNLIKE; FERTILE FRONDS NOT LEAF-LIKE IN APPEARANCE

1. SENSITIVE FERN

Onoclea sensibilis

Newfoundland to Florida, in wet meadows.

Sterile fronds.—One or two inches to three feet high, broadly triangular, deeply cut into somewhat oblong, wavy-toothed divisions, the lower ones almost reaching the midrib, the upper ones less deeply cut; *stalk* long.

Fertile fronds.—Quite unlike the sterile fronds and shorter, erect, rigid, contracted; *pinnules* rolled up into dark-green, berry-like bodies which hold the spore-cases; appearing in June or July.

This is one of our commonest ferns, growing in masses along the roadside and in wet meadows. Perfectly formed sterile fronds are found of the tiniest dimensions. Again the plant holds its own among the largest and most effective ferns. From its creeping rootstock rise the scattered fronds

54

which at times wear very light and delicate shades of green. There is nothing, however, specially fragile in the plant's appearance, and one is struck by the inappropriateness of its title. It is probable that this arose from its sensitiveness to early frosts.

Though one hesitates to differ from Dr. Eaton, who described the fertile fronds as "nearly black in color" and said that they were "not very common," and that a young botanist might "search in vain for them for a long time," my own experience has been that the fresh ones are

Sensitive Fern

very evidently green and neither scarce nor specially inconspicuous.

I have found these fertile fronds apparently full-grown in June, though usually they are assigned to a much later date. They remain standing, brown and dry, long after they have sown their spores, side by side with the fresh fronds of the following summer.

Detail *a* in Plate I represents the so-called *var. obtusilobata.* This is a form midway between the fruiting and the non-fruiting fronds. It may be looked for in situations where the fern has suffered some injury or deprivation.

2. OSTRICH FERN

Onoclea Struthiopteris

Nova Scotia to New Jersey, along streams and in moist woods. Growing in a crown, two to ten feet high.

Sterile fronds.—Broadly lance-shaped, once-pinnate; *pinnæ* divided into narrowly oblong segments which do not reach the midvein; *stalk* short, deeply channelled in front.

Fertile fronds.—Quite unlike the sterile fronds, growing in the centre of the crown formed by the sterile fronds, shorter, erect, rigid, with green, necklace-like pinnæ which hold the spore-cases; appearing in July.

I first found this plant at its best on the shore of the Hoosick River in Rensselaer County, N. Y. We had crossed a field dotted with fragrant heaps of hay and blazing in the midsummer sun, and had entered the cool shade of the trees which border the river, when suddenly I saw before me a group of ferns of tropical beauty and luxuriance. Great

PLATE I

SENSITIVE FERN
a. Var. obtusilobata

57

plume-like fronds of a rich green arched above my
head. From the midst of the circle which they
formed sprang the shorter, dark, rigid fruit-clusters.
I was fairly startled by the unexpected beauty and
regal bearing of the Ostrich Fern.

This magnificent plant luxuriates especially in the
low, rich soil which is subject to an annual overflow
from our northern rivers. Its vase-like masses of
foliage somewhat suggest the Cinnamon Fern, but
the fertile fronds of the Ostrich Fern mature in
July, some weeks later than those of its rival. They
are dark-green, while those of the Cinnamon Fern
are golden-brown. Should there be no fruiting
fronds upon the plant, the Ostrich Fern can be distinguished by the free veins with simple veinlets
(Plate II, *a*) of its pinnæ, the veins of the Cinnamon
Fern being free and its veinlets forking (Pl. III, *a*),
and by the absence of the tuft of rusty wool at the
base of the pinnæ on the under side of the frond.

The Ostrich Fern does so well under cultivation
that there is danger lest it crowd out its less aggres-
sive neighbors. It propagates chiefly by means of
underground runners. Mr. Robinson describes a
specimen which he had planted in his out-door
fernery that crawled under a tight board fence and
reappeared in the garden of his neighbor, who was
greatly astonished and equally delighted so unex-
pectedly to become the owner of the superb plant.

The Ostrich Fern, like its kinsman the Sensitive
Fern, occasionally gives birth to fronds which are
midway between its fruiting and its non-fruiting

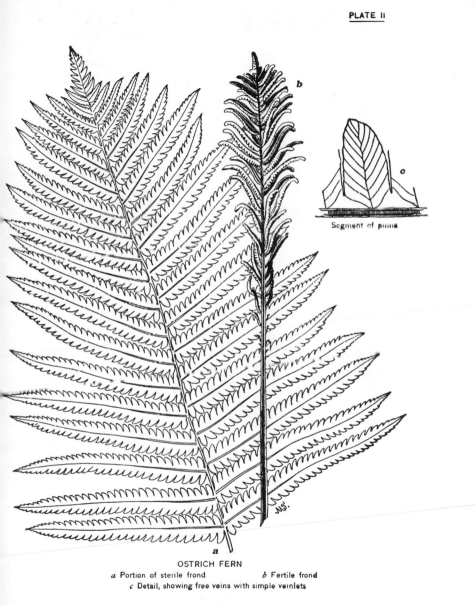

PLATE II

Segment of pinna

OSTRICH FERN
a Portion of sterile frond   *b* Fertile frond
c Detail, showing free veins with simple veinlets

59

forms. This is specially liable to occur when some injury has befallen the plant.

3. CINNAMON FERN

Osmunda cinnamomea

Nova Scotia to Florida, in swampy places. Growing in a crown, one to five feet high.

Sterile fronds.—Broadly lance-shaped, once-pinnate; *pinnæ* cut into broadly oblong divisions that do not reach the midvein, each pinna with a tuft of rusty wool at its base beneath.

Fertile fronds.—Quite unlike the sterile fronds, growing in the centre of the crown formed by the sterile fronds and usually about the same height; erect, with cinnamon-colored spore-cases.

In the form of little croziers, protected from the cold by wrappings of rusty wool, the fertile fronds of the Cinnamon Fern appear everywhere in our swamps and wet woods during the month of May. These fertile fronds, first dark-green, later cinnamon-brown, are quickly followed and encircled by the sterile ones, which grow in a tall, graceful crown. The fertile fronds soon

PLATE III

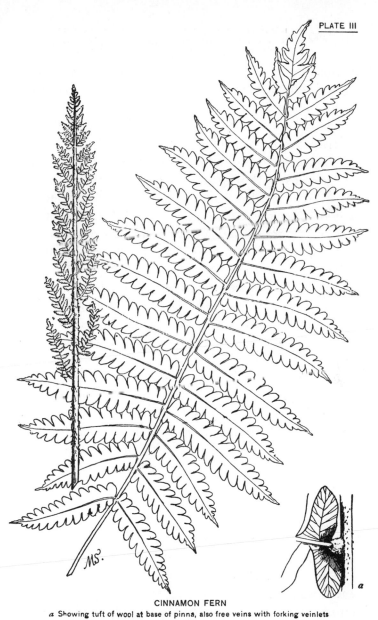

CINNAMON FERN

a Showing tuft of wool at base of pinna, also free veins with forking veinlets

61

wither, and, during the summer, may be found either clinging to the stalks of the sterile fronds or lying on the ground.

The Cinnamon Fern is often confused with the Ostrich Fern. When either plant is in fruit there is no excuse for this mistake, as the cinnamon-colored spore-cases of the former appear in May, while the dark-green fertile fronds of the latter do not ripen till July. When the fruiting fronds are absent the forked veinlets (Plate III, *a*) of the Cinnamon Fern contrast with the simple veinlets of the other plant (Plate II, *a*). Then, too, the pinnæ of the Cinnamon Fern bear tufts of rusty wool at the base beneath, the remnants of the woolly garments worn by the young fronds.

The plant is a superb one when seen at its best. Its tall sterile fronds curve gracefully outward, while the slender fruit-clusters erect themselves in the centre of the rich crown. In unfavorable conditions, when growing in dry meadows, for instance, like all the Osmundas, and indeed like most growing things, it is quite a different plant. Its green fronds become stiff and stunted, losing all their graceful curves, and its fruit-clusters huddle among them as if anxious to keep out of sight.

Var. frondosa is an occasional form in which some of the fruiting fronds have green, leaf-like pinnæ below. These abnormal fronds are most abundant on land which has been burned over.

The Cinnamon Fern is a member of the group of Osmundas, or " flowering ferns," as they are sometimes called, not of course because they really flower, but because their fruiting fronds are somewhat flower-like in appearance. There are three species of *Osmunda :* the Cinnamon Fern, *O. cinnamomea;* the Royal Fern, *O. regalis;* and the Interrupted Fern, *O. Claytoniana.* All three are beautiful and striking plants, producing their spores in May or June, and conspicuous by reason of their luxuriant growth and flower-like fruit clusters.

The Osmundas are easily cultivated, and group themselves effectively in shaded corners of the garden. They need plenty of water, and thrive best in a mixture of swamp-muck and fine loam.

4. CURLY GRASS

Schizæa pusilla

Pine barrens of New Jersey.

Sterile fronds.—Hardly an inch long, linear, slender, flattened, curly.

Fertile fronds.—Taller than the sterile fronds (three or four inches in height), slender, with from four to six pairs of fruit-bearing pinnæ in September.

Save in the herbarium I have never seen this very local little plant, which is found in certain parts of New Jersey. Gray assigns it to "low grounds, pine barrens," while Dr. Eaton attributes it to the "drier parts of sphagnous swamps among white cedars."

In my lack of personal knowledge of *Schizæa,* I venture to quote from that excellent little quarterly, the *Fern Bulletin,* the following passage from an

63

article by Mr. C. F. Saunders on *Schizæa pusilla* at home:

"S. pusilla was first collected early in this century at Quaker Bridge, N. J., about thirty-five miles east of Philadelphia. The spot is a desolate-looking place in the wildest of the 'pine barrens,' where a branch of the Atsion River flows through marshy lowlands and cedar swamps. Here, amid sedge-grasses, mosses, Lycopodiums, Droseras, and wild cranberry vines, the little treasure has been collected; but, though I have hunted for it more than once, my eyes have never been sharp enough to detect its fronds in that locality. In October of last year, however, a friend guided me to another place in New Jersey where he knew it to be growing, and there we found it. It was a small open spot in the pine barrens, low and damp. In the white sand grew patches of low grasses, mosses, Lycopodium Carolinianum, L. inundatum, and Pyxidanthera barbulata, besides several smaller ericaceous plants and some larger shrubs, such as scrub-oaks, sumacs, etc. Close by was a little stream, and just beyond that a bog. Although we knew that the Schizæa grew within a few feet of the path in which we stood, it required the closest sort of a search, with eyes at the level of our knees, before a specimen was detected. The sterile fronds (curled like corkscrews) grew in little tufts, and were more readily visible than the fertile spikes, which were less numerous, and, together with the slender stipes, were of a brown color, hardly dis-

PLATE IV

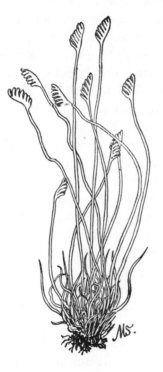

CURLY GRASS

tinguishable from the capsules of the mosses, and the maturing stems of the grasses which grew all about. Lying flat on the earth, with face within a few inches of the ground, was found the most satisfactory plan of search. Down there all the individual plants looked bigger, and a sidelong glance brought the fertile clusters more prominently into view. When the sight got accustomed to the miniature jungle quite a number of specimens were found, but the fern could hardly be said to be plentiful, and all that we gathered were within a radius of a couple of yards. This seems, indeed, to be one of those plants whose whereabouts is oftenest revealed by what we are wont to term a 'happy accident,' as, for instance, when we are lying stretched on the ground resting, or as we stoop at lunch to crack an egg on the toe of our shoe. I know of one excellent collector who spent a whole day looking for it diligently in what he thought to be a likely spot, but without success, when finally, just before the time for return came, as he was half crouching on the ground, scarcely thinking now of Schizæa, its fronds suddenly flashed upon his sight, right at his feet. The sterile fronds of Schizæa pusilla are evergreen, so that the collector may, perhaps, most readily detect it in winter, selecting days for his search when the earth is pretty clear of snow. The surrounding vegetation being at that time dead, the little corkscrew-like fronds stand out more prominently."

GROUP II

5. ROYAL FERN. FLOWERING FERN

Osmunda regalis

New Brunswick to Florida, in swampy places.   Two to five feet
high, occasionally taller.

Sterile fronds.—Twice-pinnate, *pinnæ* cut into oblong pinnules.
Fertile fronds.—Leaf-like below, *sporangia* forming bright-
brown clusters at their summits.

Perhaps this Royal or Flowering Fern is the
most beautiful member of a singularly beautiful
group.   When its smooth, pale - green sterile
fronds, grown to their full height, form a graceful crown which encircles the fertile fronds, it is
truly a regal-looking plant.   These fertile fronds

67

Royal Fern

are leaf-like below, and are tipped above with their flower-like fruit-clusters.

Like its kinsmen, the Royal Fern appears in May in our wet woods and fields. The delicate little croziers uncurl with dainty grace, the plants which grow in the open among the yellow stars of the early crow-foot, and the white clusters of the spring cress being so tinged with red that they suffuse the meadows with warm color.

Though one of our tallest ferns, with us it never reaches the ten or eleven feet with which it is credited in Great Britain. The tallest plants I have found fall short of six feet. Occasionally we see large tracts of land covered with mature plants that lack a foot or more of the two feet given as the minimum height. This tendency to

PLATE V

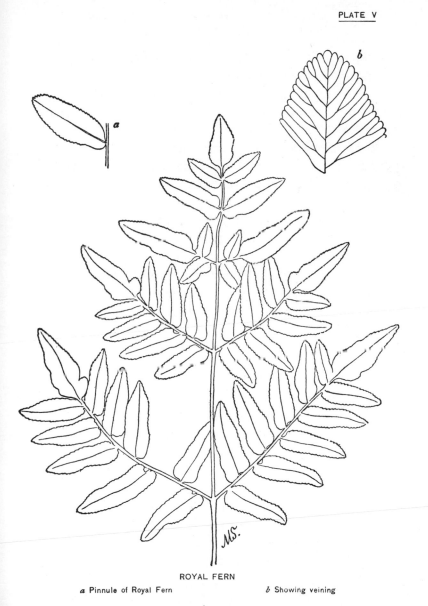

ROYAL FERN

a Pinnule of Royal Fern   *b* Showing veining

depauperization one notices especially in dry marshes near the sea.

To the Royal Fern the old herbalists attributed many valuable qualities. One old writer, who calls it the " Water Fern," says : " This hath all the virtues mentioned in other ferns, and is much more effective than they both for inward and outward griefs, and is accounted good for wounds, bruises, and the like."

The title " flowering fern " sometimes misleads those who are so unfamiliar with the habits of ferns as to imagine that they ever flower. That it really is descriptive was proved to me only a few weeks ago when I received a pressed specimen of a fertile frond accompanied by the request to inform the writer as to the name of the flower inclosed, which seemed to him to belong to the Sumach family.

The origin of the generic name *Osmunda* seems somewhat obscure. It is said to be derived from Osmunder, the Saxon Thor. In his Herbal Gerarde tells us that *Osmunda regalis* was formerly called " Osmund, the Waterman," in allusion, perhaps, to its liking for a home in the marshes. One legend claims that a certain Osmund, living at Loch Tyne, saved his wife and child from the inimical Danes by hiding them upon an island among masses of flowering ferns, and that in after years the child so shielded named the stately plants after her father.

The following lines from Wordsworth point to
still another origin of the generic name :

> " — often, trifling with a privilege
> Alike indulged to all, we paused, one now,
> And now the other, to point out, perchance
> To pluck, some flower, or water-weed, too fair
> Either to be divided from the place
> On which it grew, or to be left alone
> To its own beauty. Many such there are,
> Fair ferns and flowers, and chiefly that tall fern,
> So stately, of the Queen Osmunda named ;
> Plant lovelier, in its own retired abode
> On Grasmere's beach, than Naiad by the side
> Of Grecian brook, or Lady of the Mere,
> Sole-sitting by the shores of old romance."

The Royal Fern may be cultivated easily in deep
mounds of rich soil shielded somewhat from the
sun.

6. INTERRUPTED FERN

Osmunda Claytoniana

Newfoundland to North Carolina, in swampy places. Two to four feet high.

Sterile fronds.—Oblong-lanceolate, once-pinnate, *pinnæ* cut into oblong, obtuse divisions, *without* a tuft of wool at the base of each pinna.

Fertile fronds.—Taller than the sterile, leaf-like above and below, some of the middle pinnæ fruit-bearing.

The Interrupted Fern makes its appearance in the woods and meadows and along the roadsides in May. It fruits as it unfolds.

At first the fruiting pinnæ are almost black. Later they become golden-green, and after the spores are discharged they turn brown. They are noticeable all summer, and serve to identify the plant at once.

In the absence of the fertile fronds it is often difficult to distinguish between the Cinnamon Fern and the Interrupted Fern.

The sterile fronds of the Interrupted Fern are usually less erect, curving outward much more noticeably than those of the Cinnamon Fern. Then, too, its pinnæ are cut into segments that are more obtuse, and the whole effect of the frond is more stubby.

But the most distinguishing feature of all is the tuft of rusty wool which clings to the base of each pinna of the sterile fronds of the Cinnamon Fern. These tufts we do not find in the Interrupted Fern, though both plants come into the world warmly wrapped in wool.

The Interrupted Fern is a peculiarly graceful plant.

72

PLATE VI

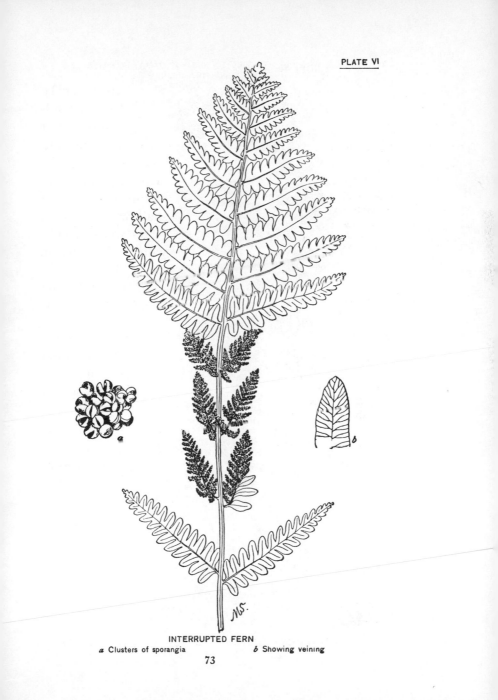

INTERRUPTED FERN

a Clusters of sporangia   *b* Showing veining

73

Its fertile
fronds, stand-
ing quite erect
below but curving
outward above the
fruiting pinnæ, are
set in a somewhat
shallow vase formed
by the sterile fronds,
which fall away in
every direction.

In the fall the
fronds turn yel-
low, and
at times
are so
brilliant
that
they
flood the
woods
with gold-
en light.

Like the
other Os-
mundas,
the Inter-
rupted
Fern is
easily cul-
tivated.

Interrupted Fern

7. CLIMBING FERN. CREEPING FERN. HARTFORD FERN

Lygodium palmatum

Massachusetts and southward, in moist
thickets and open woods. Stalks
slender and twining.

Fronds.—Climbing and twining, one
to three feet long, divided into lobed,
rounded, heart - shaped, short - stalked
segments; *fruit - clusters*, growing at
the summit of the frond, ripening in
September.

The Climbing Fern is still found
occasionally in moist thickets and
open woods from Massachusetts southward,
but at one time it was picked so reck-
lessly for decorative purposes that it was almost
exterminated.

In 1869 the legislature of Connecticut passed for
its protection a special law which was embodied in
the revision of the statutes of 1875, "perhaps the

only instance in statute law," Dr. Eaton remarks, "where a plant has received special legal protection solely on account of its beauty."

I have never seen the plant growing, but remember that when a child my home in New York was abundantly decorated with the pressed fronds which

had been brought from Hartford for the purpose. Even in that lifeless condition their grace and beauty made a deep impression on my mind.

Mr. Saunders has described it as he found it growing in company with *Schizæa*, in the New Jersey pine barrens :

Part of fertile pinnule

" Lygodium palmatum . . . is one of the loveliest of American plants, with twining stem adorned with palmate leaflets, bearing small resemblance to the popular idea of a fern. It loves the shaded, mossy banks of the quiet streams whose cool, clear, amber waters, murmuring over beds of pure white sand, are so characteristic of the pine country. There the graceful fronds are to be found, sometimes clambering a yard high over the bushes and cat-briers ; sometimes trailing down the bank until their tips touch the surface of the water.

" The Lygodium is reckoned among the rare plants of the region—though often growing in good-sized patches when found at all—and is getting rarer. Many of the localities which knew it once now know it no more, both because of the depredations of ruthless collectors, and, to some extent, probably, the ravages of fire. The plant is in its prime in early fall, but may be looked for up to the time of killing frosts."

8. ADDER'S TONGUE

Ophioglossum vulgatum

Canada to New Jersey and Kentucky, in moist meadows. Two inches to one foot high.

Sterile portion.—An ovate, fleshy leaf.
Fertile portion.—A simple spike, usually long-stalked.

The unprofessional fern collector is likely to agree with Gray in considering the Adder's Tongue "not common." Many botanists, however, believe the plant to be "overlooked rather than rare." In an article on *O. vulgatum*, which appeared some years ago in the *Fern Bulletin*, Mr. A. A. Eaton writes:

"Previous to 1895 Ophioglossum vulgatum was unknown to me, and was considered very rare, only two localities being known in Essex County, Mass. Early in the year a friend gave me two specimens. From these I got an idea of how the thing looked. On the 11th of last July, while collecting Habenaria lacera in a 'bound-out' mowing field, I was delighted to notice a spike of fruit in the grass. A search revealed about sixty, just right to collect, with many unfruitful specimens. A few days later,

while raking in a similar locality, I found several,
within a stone's throw of the house, demonstrating
again the well-known fact that a thing once seen is
easily discovered again.   On the 23d of last August,
while riding on my bicycle, I noticed a field that
appeared to be the right locality, and an investigation showed an abundance of them.   I subsequently
found it in another place.   This year, on May 28th,
I found it in another locality just as it was coming
up, and I have since found three others.   I consider it abundant here, only appearing rare because
growing hidden in fine grass in old mowing fields,
after the red top and timothy have died out, and the
finer species of Carex are coming in.   A good index plant is the Habenaria quoted.   I have never
found it except when associated with this plant,
on a cold, heavy soil.   The leaf is usually hidden,
or, if not, is easily passed by for Maianthemum or
Pogonia."

In the "Grete Herbal" of Gerarde we read that
"the leaves of Adder's Tongue stamped in a stone
mortar, and boiled in oyle olive unto the consump-
tion of the juice, and until the herbs be dried and
parched and then strained, will yeelde most excellent
greene oyle or rather a balsame for greene wounds
comparable to oyle of St. John's-wort if it do not
farre surpasse it."

It is said that "Adder's Spear Ointment," made
from the fresh fronds of this plant is still used for
wounds in English villages.

The Adder's Tongue was believed formerly to

PLATE VII

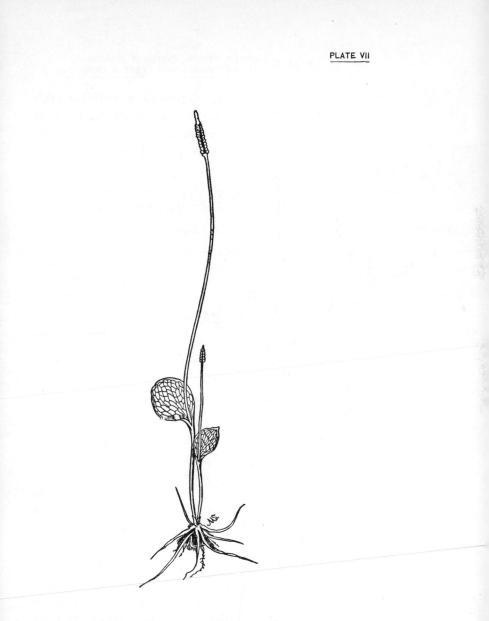

ADDER'S TONGUE

have poisonous qualities, which not only injured the cattle that fed upon it, but destroyed the grass in which it grew.

9. RATTLESNAKE FERN. VIRGINIA GRAPE FERN

Botrychium Virginianum

Nova Scotia to Florida, in rich woods. One or two feet high, at times much smaller, when it becomes *B. gracile.*

Sterile portion.— Usually broader than long, spreading, with three main divisions which are cut into many smaller segments, thin, set close to the stem about half way up.

Fertile portion.— Long-stalked, more than once-pinnate.

On our rambles through the woods we are more likely to encounter the Rattlesnake Fern than any other member of the *Botrychium* group. It fruits in early sum-

Rattlesnake Fern

80

mer, but the withered fertile portion may be found upon the plant much later in the year. Its frequent companions are the Spinulose Shield Fern, the Christmas Fern, the Silvery Spleenwort, and the Maidenhair.

10. TERNATE GRAPE FERN

Botrychium ternatum or *dissectum*

Nova Scotia to Florida, in moist meadows.   A few inches to more than a foot high.

Sterile portion.—Broadly triangular, the three main divisions cut again into many segments, on a separate stalk from near the base of the plant, fleshy.

Fertile portion.—Erect, usually considerably taller than non-fruiting segment, more than once-pinnate.

Sporangia of Botrychium

Of late some doubt has existed as to whether *B. ternatum* has been actually found in this country, although the standard Floras give no evidence of this uncertainty. Dr. Underwood is convinced that the true *B. ternatum* is found only in Japan and China, and that our species is really *B. dissectum*, a species, not a variety. He says that this species is very common in the vicinity of New York City, and thence southward and westward; that it is also found in various parts of New England; that it reaches its fullest development in moist,

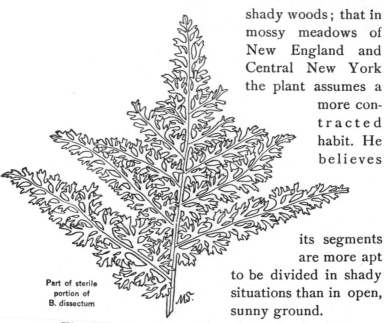

Part of sterile
portion of
B. dissectum

shady woods; that in mossy meadows of New England and Central New York the plant assumes a more contracted habit. He believes its segments are more apt to be divided in shady situations than in open, sunny ground.

The Ternate Grape Fern fruits in the fall.

11. LITTLE GRAPE FERN

Botrychium simplex

Canada to Maryland, in moist woods and in fields. Two to four
inches high, rarely a little taller.

Sterile portion.—Somewhat oblong, more or less lobed, occasionally 3–7 divided, usually short-stalked from near the middle of the plant, thick and fleshy.

Fertile portion.—Either simple or once or twice-pinnate, taller than the sterile portion.

This little plant is sufficiently rare to rejoice the heart of the fern hunter who is so fortunate as to

82

PLATE VI

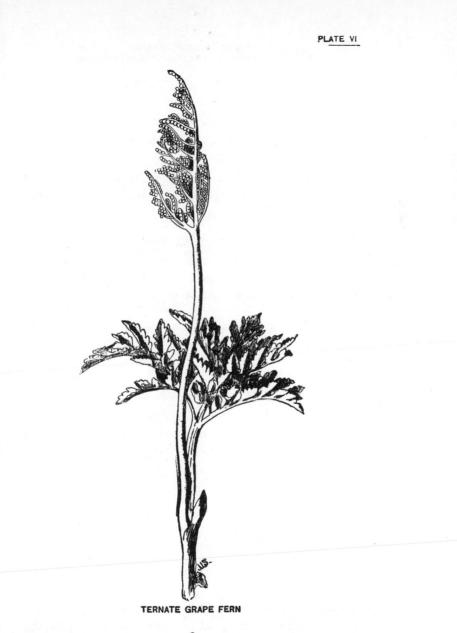

TERNATE GRAPE FERN

stumble upon it by chance or to trace it to its chosen haunts.

It is generally considered an inhabitant of moist woods and meadows, though Mr. Pringle describes it as "abundantly scattered over Vermont, its habitat usually poor soil, especially knolls of hill pastures," and Mr. Dodge assigns it to "dry fields." It fruits in May or June.

12. MOONWORT

Botrychium Lunaria

Newfoundland to Connecticut and Central New York, in dry pastures.   Three inches to nearly one foot high.   A very fleshy plant.

Sterile portion.—Oblong, cut into several fan-shaped fleshy divisions, growing close to the stem about the middle of the plant.

Fertile portion.—Branching, long-stalked, usually the same height as or taller than the sterile portion.

The Moonwort is another of our rare little plants. It grows usually in dry pastures, fruiting in July.

Formerly it was accredited with various magic powers.   Gathered by moonlight, it was said to "do wonders."   The English poet Drayton refers to the Moonwort as "Lunary"·

> "Then sprinkled she the juice of rue
> With nine drops of the midnight dew
> From Lunary distilling."

Gerarde mentions its use by alchemists, who called it Martagon.   In the work of Coles, an early writer on plants, we read: "It is said, yea, and believed by many that Moonwort will open the

PLATE IX

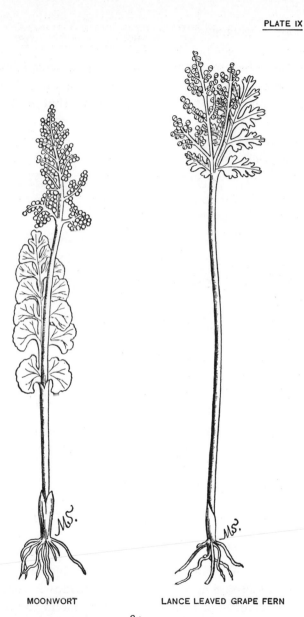

MOONWORT   LANCE LEAVED GRAPE FERN

locks wherewith dwelling-houses are made fast, if it be put into the keyhole ; as also that it will loosen . . . shoes from those horses' feet that go on the places where it grows."

It is to the Moonwort that Withers alludes in the following lines :

> " There is an herb, some say, whose vertue's such
> It in the pasture, only with a touch
> Unshoes the new-shod steed."

13. MATRICARY GRAPE FERN

Botrychium matricariæfolium

Nova Scotia to New Jersey, in woods and wet meadows. Two inches to one foot high.

Sterile portion.—Once or twice divided, sometimes very fleshy, growing high up on the stem.
Fertile portion.—With several branched pinnæ.

This plant is found, often in the companionship of *B. Virginianum*, in woods and wet meadows, not farther south than New Jersey. It fruits in summer.

14. LANCE-LEAVED GRAPE FERN

Botrychium lanceolatum

Nova Scotia to New Jersey, in woods and meadows. Two to nine inches high.

Sterile portion.—Triangular, twice-pinnatifid, with somewhat lance-shaped segments, hardly fleshy, set close to the top of the common stalk.
Fertile portion.—Branching.

Like the Matricary Grape Fern, this plant is found in the woods and wet meadows from Nova Scotia to New Jersey. It fruits also in summer.

GROUP III

FERTILE FRONDS UNIFORMLY SOMEWHAT LEAF-LIKE IN
APPEARANCE, YET DIFFERING NOTICEABLY FROM
STERILE FRONDS

15. SLENDER CLIFF BRAKE

Pellæa gracilis (P. Stelleri)

Labrador to Pennsylvania, usually on sheltered rocks, preferring limestone. Two to five inches long, with straw-colored or pale-brown stalks, slightly chaffy below.

Fronds.—Delicate, with few pinnæ ; *pinnæ*, the lower ones once or twice parted into 3–5 divisions, those of the fertile frond oblong or linear-oblong, sparingly incised, of the sterile frond ovate or obovate, toothed or incised ; *sporangia* bordering the pinnæ of the fertile frond, covered by a broad and usually continuous general *indusium*, formed by the reflexed margin of the *pinnule.*

The first time I found the Slender Cliff Brake was one July day in Central New York, under the kind guidance of an enthusiastic fern collector. A rather perilous climb along the sides of a thickly wooded glen brought us to a spot where our only security lay in clinging to the trees, which, like our-

87

selves, had obtained doubtful standing-room. In a pocket in the limestone just above us I was shown a very brown and withered little plant which only the closest scrutiny in combination with a certain amount of foreknowledge could identify as the Slender Cliff Brake. The season had been a dry one and the plant had perished, I fancy, for lack of water, in spite of the stream which plunged from the top of the cliffs close by, almost near enough, it

seemed to me, to moisten with its spray our hot cheeks.

Later in the season I found more promising though not altogether satisfactory specimens of this plant growing in other rocky crevices of the same deep glen, in the neighborhood of the Maidenhair Spleenwort, the Walking Leaf, and the Bulblet Bladder Fern.

Portion of fertile frond

My sister tells me that late in August on the cliffs which border the St. Lawrence River, refreshed by the myriad streams which leap or trickle down their sides, under the hanging roots of trees, close to clusters of quivering harebells and pale tufts of the Brittle Bladder Fern, the Slender Cliff Brake grows in profusion, its delicate fronds rippling over one another so closely that at times they give the effect of a long, luxuriant moss. On most occasions, in these soft beds of foliage, she found the fertile fronds, which are far more slender and unusual looking than the sterile, largely predominating, though at times a patch would be

made up chiefly of the sterile fronds. These somewhat resemble the Brittle Bladder Fern in whose
company they are seen so often.

Slender Cliff Brake

16. PURPLE CLIFF BRAKE

Pellæa atropurpurea

Canada to Georgia and westward, usually on limestone cliffs; with wiry purplish stalks.

Fertile fronds.—Six to twenty inches high, leathery, bluish-green, pale underneath, once, or below twice, pinnate; *pinnæ*, upper ones long and narrow, lower ones usually with one to four pairs of broadly linear *pinnules; sporangia* bordering the pinnæ, bright brown at maturity; *indusium* formed by the reflexed margin of the frond.

Sterile fronds.—Usually much smaller than the fertile and less abundant; *pinnæ* oblong, entire, or slightly toothed.

The Purple Cliff Brake is one of the plants that rejoice in un-get-at-able and perilous situations. Although its range is wider than that of many ferns, this choice of inconvenient localities, joined to the fact that it is not a common plant, renders it likely that unless you pay it the compliment of a special expedition in its honor you will never add it to the list of your fern acquaintances.

But when all is said we are inestimably in debt to the plants so rare or so exclusive as to entice us out of our usual haunts into theirs. Not only do they draw us away from our books, out of our houses, but off the well-known road and the trodden path into unfamiliar woods which stand ready to reveal fresh treasures, across distant pastures where the fragrant wind blows away the memory of small anxieties, up into the hills from whose summits we get new views.

Although the Purple Cliff Brake grows, I believe,

PLATE X

PURPLE CLIFF BRAKE
a Portion of fertile frond

within fifteen miles of my home in Albany, I never saw the plant until this summer some hundred miles nearer the centre of the State. During a morning call I chanced to mention that I was anxious to find two or three ferns which were said to grow in the neighborhood. My hostess told me that twenty-five years before, on some limestone cliffs about eight miles away, she had found two unknown ferns which had been classified and labelled by a botanical friend. Excusing herself she left me and soon returned with carefully pressed specimens of the Purple Cliff Brake and the little Rue Spleenwort, the two ferns I was most eager to find. Such moments as I experienced then of long-deferred but peculiar satisfaction go far toward making one an apostle of hobbies. My pleasure was increased by the kind offer to guide me to the spot which had yielded the specimens.

One morning soon after we were set down at the little railway station from which we purposed to walk to the already-mentioned cliffs. We were not without misgivings as we followed an indefinite path across some limestone quarries, for a plant may easily disappear from a given station in the course of twenty-five years. In a few moments the so-called path disappeared in a fringe of bushes which evidently marked the beginning of a precipitous descent. Cautiously clinging to whatever we could lay hold of, bushes, roots of trees or imbedded rocks, we climbed over the cliff's side, still following the semblance of a path. On our left a stream plunged

nearly two hundred feet into the ravine below.   For
some distance the eye could follow its silver course,
then it disappeared beneath the arching trees.   On
our right, many miles beyond, through the blue haze
which hung over the distant valley, we could see the
lake to which the stream was hurrying.

We could not surrender ourselves with comfort
to the beauty of the outlook, as our surroundings
were not such as to put us altogether at ease.   Overhead hung great rocks, so cracked and seamed and
shattered as to threaten a complete downfall, while
beneath our feet the path which led along the face
of the cliff crumbled away, so that it was difficult
in places to obtain any foothold.   Having passed
the more perilous spots, however, we became accustomed to the situation and turned our attention to
the unpromising wall of rock which rose beside us.
From its crevices hung graceful festoons of Bulblet
Bladder Fern, and apparently nothing but Bulblet
Bladder Fern.   But soon one of the party gave a
cry and pointed in triumph to a bluish-green cluster
of foliage which sprang from a shallow pocket overhead.   Even though one had not seen the plant
before, there was no mistaking the wiry purplish
stalks, the leathery, pinnately parted, blue-green
fronds, and, above all, the marginal rows of bright
brown sporangia peculiar to the Purple Cliff Brake.
Soon after we found several other plants, all of them
decidedly scraggly in appearance, with but few
green fronds and many leafless stalks.   Occasionally a small sterile frond, with broader, more oblong

93

pinnæ, could be seen, but these were in the minority.
A number of very young plants, with little, heart-
shaped leaves altogether unlike the mature fronds,
were wedged in neighboring crannies.

As our eyes grew more accustomed to the con-
tour and coloring of the cliffs, the success of the
day was completed by the discovery of several
specimens of the little Rue Spleenwort with tiny
fronds flattened against the rock.

When next I saw the Purple Cliff Brake it
seemed to me quite a different fern from the rather
awkward plant, the mere sight of which I had welcomed so eagerly that any unfavorable criticism of
its appearance seems ungrateful.

Again it sprang from limestone cliffs, even more
remote and inaccessible though less dangerous than
those where I saw it first. These cliffs were so
shattered in places that the broken fragments lay in
heaps at their base and on the projecting ledges.
Here and there a great shaft of rock had broken
away and stood like the turret of a castle or the
bastion of a fort. Among the shattered fragments
high up on the cliff's side the Purple Cliff Brake
grew in a luxuriant profusion that was amazing in
view of the surroundings. The rigid, erect fronds
formed large tufts of greenish-gray foliage that, at
a little distance, so blended with their rocky background as to be almost indistinguishable. The
fronds usually were much more compound than
those I had seen a few weeks before. The separate
plants had a vigorous, bushy appearance that did

not suggest the same species. Many of the pinnæ were so turned as to display the ripe sporangia, which formed a bright-brown border to the pale, slender divisions. Here, too, the small sterile fronds were very rare.

Growing from the broken rocks in among the Purple Cliff Brake were thrifty little tufts of the Maidenhair Spleenwort. This tiny plant seemed to have forgotten its shyness and to have forsworn its love for moist, shaded, mossy rocks. It ventured boldly out upon these barren cliffs, exposing itself to the fierce glare of the sun and to every blast of wind, and holding itself upright with a saucy self-assurance that seemed strangely at variance with its nature.

Near by a single patch of the Walking Leaf climbed up the face of the cliff, while, perhaps strangest of all, from the decaying trunk of a tree, which lay prostrate among the rocks, sprang a single small but perfect plant of the Ebony Spleenwort, a fern which was a complete stranger in this locality, so far as I could learn.

a.g.s.

More compound frond
of Purple Cliff Brake

Sterile frond

95

17. CHRISTMAS FERN

Aspidium acrostichoides (*Dryopteris acrostichoides*)

New Brunswick to Florida, in rocky woods. One to two and a half feet high, with very chaffy stalks.

Fronds.—Lance-shaped, once-pinnate, fertile fronds contracted toward the summit; *pinnæ* narrowly lance-shaped, half halberd-shaped at the slightly stalked base, bristly-toothed, the upper ones on the fertile fronds contracted and smaller; *fruit-dots* round, close, confluent with age, nearly covering the under surface of the fertile pinnæ; *indusium* orbicular, fixed by the depressed centre.

Of our evergreen ferns this is the best fitted to serve as a decoration in winter. No other fern has such deep-green, highly polished fronds. They need only a mixture of red berries to become a close rival to the holly at Christmas time.

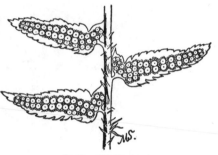

Portion of fertile frond

Wrapped in a garment of brown scales, the young fronds of the Christmas Fern are sent into the world early in the spring. When we go to the woods in April to look for arbutus, or to listen to the first songs of the robin and the bluebird, we notice that last year's fronds are still fresh and green. Low down among them, curled up like tawny caterpillars, are the young fronds. The arbutus will have made way for pink and blue and white hepaticas, for starry bloodroot, and for tremulous anemones; thrushes and orioles will have joined the robins and the bluebirds before these new-comers present much of an appearance. W h e n the tender, delicately green fronds are first unrolled they contrast strongly w i t h their polished, d a r k - g r e e n, leathery companions.

In this plant the difference is quite conspicuous between the fertile and the sterile fronds. The sterile ones are shorter and apparently broader, while the fertile are tall, slender, and noticeably contracted by the abundantly fruiting pinnæ near the apex.

Christmas Fern

18. NARROW-LEAVED SPLEEN-
WORT

Asplenium angustifolium

Canada to Kentucky, in moist woods. Two
to four feet high.

Sterile fronds. — Thin, smooth, lance-
shaped, perishable, once-pinnate.
Fertile fronds.—Taller, narrower, longer-
stalked; *pinnæ* more narrowly lance-shaped
than on sterile fronds; *fruit-dots* linear, a
row on each side the midvein; *indusium*
slightly convex.

If we make an expedition to the
woods early in July we may, perhaps, find some plants of the Narrow-leaved Spleenwort.   At this
season they are specially attract-
ive, with smooth, delicate, pale-green fronds, so recently unfolded as to be full of little undulations,
which they lose more or less at maturity, and
which are as indicative of youth as the curves and
dimples of a baby.

PLATE XI

NARROW-LEAVED SPLEENWORT
a Magnified pinna of fertile frond

99

Late in August the plant has reached a stately height, perhaps of three or four feet. The fronds are still smooth and delicate to a degree unusual even in ferns. But they wear a deeper green, and their texture seems a trifle more substantial. Occasionally, though rarely in the deeper woods, we find a frond which is conspicuously longer-stalked, taller, narrower than the others, with pinnæ more distant and more contracted. A glance at its lower surface discovers double rows of brown, linear fruit-dots.

Though one of the largest of its tribe, the Narrow-leaved Spleenwort suggests greater fragility, a keener sensitiveness to uncongenial conditions, than any other of our native ferns. A storm which leaves the other inhabitants of the forest almost untouched beats down its fronds, tender and perishable even in maturity.

This very fragility, accompanied as it is with beauty of form and color, in the midst of the somewhat coarse and hardy growth of the August woods, lends the plant a peculiar charm.

I find it growing beneath great basswoods, lichen-spotted beeches, and sugar maples with trunks branchless for fifty feet, soaring like huge shipmasts into the blue above.

Almost the only flowers in its neighborhood, for in midsummer wood-flowers are rare, are the tiny pink blossoms of the herb Robert, that invincible little plant which never wearies in well-doing, but persists in flowering from June till October, the violet-blue heads of the almost equally untiring self-heal and the yellow pitchers of the pale touch-me-not or jewel-weed. This plant, a close relative of the more southern and better known spotted touch-me-not, grows in great patches almost in the heart of the woods. The lack of flowers is somewhat atoned for by the coral clusters of the red baneberry and the black-spotted, china-like fruit of the white baneberry.

But ferns chiefly abound in these woods. Everywhere I notice the thin, spreading frond and withered fruit-cluster of the Rattlesnake Fern, in my experience the most ubiquitous member of the *Botrychium* group. More or less frequent are graceful crowns of the Spinulose Shield Fern, slender shining fronds of Christmas Fern, dull-green groups of Silvery Spleenwort and stately plumes of Goldie's Fern. As we draw near the wood's border, where the yellow sunlit fields of grain shine between the tall maple shafts, we push aside umbrella-like Brakes. At the very limits of the woods, close against the rails, grows the sweet-scented *Dicksonia*.

19. NET-VEINED CHAIN FERN

Woodwardia angustifolia

Swampy places from Maine to Florida, in wet woods near the coast.

Sterile fronds.—Twelve to eighteen inches high, pinnatifid with
minutely toothed divisions united by a broad wing.

Fertile fronds.—Taller than the sterile, once-pinnate; *pinnæ*
much contracted; *fruit-dots* in a single row each side of the sec-
ondary midribs; *indusium* fixed by its outer margin, opening on
the side next the midrib.

The Woodwardias are associated in my mind
with sea-air, pine-trees, and the flat, sandy country

near Buzzard's Bay, Mass. Both
species were met with in one walk
not far from the shore.

A little stream, scarcely
more than a ditch, divided
an open, sunny meadow
from a bit of evergreen
wood, and on the steep

banks of this runlet grew the bright fronds
of *Woodwardia angustifolia*, giving at first
glance somewhat the impression of *Onoclea sensibilis.* The fronds of both are described as pinnatifid, and in this *Woodwardia* we find the divisions minutely
toothed (*a*), giving them a rough outline
which is wanting in *Onoclea sensibilis.*
These are the sterile fronds. Among them
and taller than they are the fertile fronds
with very narrow divisions, covered on the lower
side with the chains of fruit-dots (*b*).

PLATE XII

NET-VEINED CHAIN FERN
103

It is a handsome fern and very satisfactory to the novice in fern hunting, because, taking fertile and sterile fronds together, it cannot be confused with any other species.

Crossing the tiny stream, a path dim with the shade of low, dense evergreens and soft and elastic underfoot from their fallen leaves, leads through the woods. Here among the partridge-vine that runs over the rocks, growing from the soft, spongy soil, are groups of the sterile fronds only of this *Woodwardia*, charming little clumps of fresh green that invite one to dig them up and plant them in boxes or baskets for decorative purposes.

GROUP IV

20. BRAKE. BRACKEN. EAGLE FERN

Pteris aquilina

Almost throughout North America, in dry, somewhat open places. One to two feet high ordinarily, occasionally much higher.

Fronds.—Solitary, one to two feet wide, cut into three primary divisions which are twice-pinnate, widely spreading at the summit of an erect, stout stalk; *sporangia* borne in a continuous line along the lower margin of the frond; *indusium* formed by the reflexed edge of the frond.

Of all ferns the Brake is the most widely distributed. It occurs in one form or another in all parts of the world. With us it grows commonly from one to two feet high, occasionally higher. In Oregon it attains a height of six or seven feet, in the Andes of fourteen feet.

It is a vigorous and often a beautiful and striking plant, growing abundantly on sunny hillsides and in open woods.

105

In the spring or early summer its solitary spreading frond, light-green and delicate in color, might
almost be confused with the Oak Fern.   Later its
green takes on a dark, dull shade, and its general
aspect becomes more
hardy   than   that   of
any other fern.

The B r a k e is be-

lieved to be the
"fearn" of the early
Saxons and to have given this pre-
fix to many English towns and villages, such as Fearnhow or Farnhow, Farningham, etc.

It is one of the few ferns mentioned by name in general literature.   In the "Lady of the Lake"
it is alluded to in the song of the heir of Armandave:

Brake

"The heath this night must be my bed,
The Bracken curtain for my head."

Pteris esculenta, a variety of our Brake, is said to have been one of the chief articles of food in New Zealand. It was called "fern-root," and in Dr. Thompson's "Story of New Zealand" is spoken of as follows: "This food is celebrated in song, and the young women, in laying before travellers baskets of cooked fern-root, chant: 'What shall be our food? Shall shellfish and fern-root? That is the root of the earth; that is the food to satisfy a man; the tongues grow by reason of the licking, as if it were the tongue of a dog.'"

The titles Brake and Bracken are not always confined to their lawful owner. Frequently they are applied to any large ferns, such as the Osmundas, or even to such superficially fern-like plants as *Myrica asplenifolia*, the so-called sweet fern.

There is a difference of opinion as to the origin of the plant's scientific name, which signifies eagle

Pinnule of Brake showing reflexed edges

wing. Some suppose it to be derived from the outline of the heraldic eagle which has been seen by the imaginative in a cross-section of the young stalk. It seems more likely that a resemblance has been fancied between the spreading frond and the plumage of an eagle.

The Brake turns brown in autumn, but does not wither away till the following year.

21. MAIDENHAIR

Adiantum pedatum

Nova Scotia to British Columbia, south to Georgia and Arkansas, in moist woods.   Ten to eighteen inches high.

Fronds.—Forked at the summit of the slender black and polished stalk, the recurved branches bearing on one side several slender, spreading pinnate divisions ; *pinnules* obliquely triangular-oblong ; *sporangia* in short fruit-dots on the under margin of a lobe of the frond ; *indusium* formed by the reflexed lobe or tooth of the frond.

For purposes of identification it would seem almost superfluous to describe the Maidenhair, a

plant which probably is more generally appreciated than all the rest of the ferns together.   Yet, strangely enough, it is confused constantly with other plants and with plants which are not ferns.

Perhaps the early meadow rue is the plant most commonly mistaken for the Maidenhair.   While it does not suggest strikingly our eastern fern, its lobed and rounded

A pinna of Maidenhair

leaflets bear a likeness to certain species native to other parts of the country, notably to *A. Capillus-Veneris*, the Venus-hair Fern of the southern States.

108

But it is not easy to convince a friend that he has
made a mistake in this regard.   You chance to be
driving by a bank overgrown with the early meadow rue when he calls your attention to the unusual
abundance of Maidenhair in the neighborhood.   To
his rather indignant surprise you suggest that the
plant he saw was not Maidenhair, but the early
meadow rue.   If he have the least reverence for
your botanical attainments he grudgingly admits
that possibly it was not the ordinary Maidenhair,
but maintains stoutly that it was a more uncommon species which abounds in his especial neighborhood.   If truly diplomatic you hold your peace
and change the subject, but
if possessed by a torment-
ing love of truth which is
always getting you into
trouble, you state sadly but
firmly that our northeastern States have but one species of Maidenhair, and that

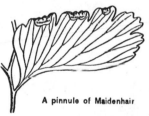

A pinnule of Maidenhair

it is more than improbable that the favored neighborhood of his home (for it is always an unusually rich
locality) offers another.   The result of this discussion is that mentally you are pronounced both con-
ceited and pig-headed.   For a few weeks the plants
in question are passed without comment, but by another summer the rich growth of Maidenhair is again
proudly exhibited.   Only in one way can you save
your reputation and possibly convince your friend.
When correcting him, if you glibly remark that

Adiantum pedatum, our northeastern Maidenhair, is the only species which has been found in this part of the country, that *A. Capillus-Veneris,* the Maidenhair which somewhat resembles the early meadow rue, can hardly be found north of Virginia, while *A. tenerum* is found only in Florida, and *A. emarginatum* is confined to the Pacific coast, you will have redeemed yourself, not

Maidenhair

from the stigma of conceit, far from it, but from that of error. The glib utterance of Latin names is attended with a strange power of silencing your opponent and filling him with a sort of grudging belief in your scientific attainments.

The truth is that the average layman who takes an interest in plants is as sensitive regarding the Maidenhair as he is about his recognition of an orchid. By way of warning what more need be said ?

Though the Maidenhair has a wide range and grows abundantly in many localities, it possesses a quality of aloofness which adds to its charm. Even in neighborhoods where it grows profusely, it rarely crowds to the roadside or becomes the companion of your daily walks. Its chosen haunts are dim, moist hollows in the woods or shaded hill-sides sloping to the river. In such retreats you find the feathery fronds tremulous on their black, glistening stalks, and in their neighborhood you find also the very spirit of the woods.

Despite its apparent fragility, the Maidenhair is not difficult to cultivate if provided with sufficient shade and moisture.

22. HAIRY LIP FERN

Cheilanthes vestita (C. lanosa)

Growing on rocks, Southern New York to Georgia.   Six to fifteen
inches high, with brown and shining stalks.

Fronds.—Oblong-lance-shaped, rough with rusty hairs, twice-
pinnate; *pinnæ* rather distant, triangular-ovate, cut into oblong,
more or less incised pinnules; *fruit-dots* roundish; *indusium*
formed by the reflexed margins of the lobes which are pushed back
by the matured sporangia.

Till a few years ago the most northern station for
the Hairy Lip Fern was supposed to be within the
limits of New York City. The plant was discovered, in 1866 or 1867, on Manhattan Island, near Fort
Tryon, growing on rocks with an eastern exposure.
If one should visit this station to-day he would find
himself at 196th Street, in the city of New York,
some two hundred and thirty-three yards west of
the Kingsbridge road, and I fear there would be no
trace of this to us rare fern.

Since then the plant has been discovered close to
the Hudson River at Poughkeepsie.

Its narrowly oblong, dull-green fronds, more or
less covered with red-brown hairs, which give it a
somewhat rusty appearance, spring from the clefts
and ledges of rocks.

PLATE XIII

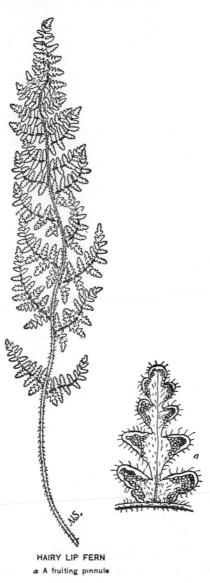

HAIRY LIP FERN

a A fruiting pinnule

23. HAY-SCENTED FERN

Dicksonia pilosiuscula (*D. punctilobula*)

Two to three feet high; hill-sides, meadows, and thickets from
Canada to Tennessee.

Fronds.—Ovate-lance-shaped, long-tapering, pale-green, thin
and very delicate in texture, slightly glandular and hairy, usually
thrice-pinnatifid ; *pinnæ* lance-shaped, pointed, repeating in miniature outline of frond ; *pinnules* cut again into short and obtuse
lobes or segments ; *fruit-dots* each on an elevated globular receptacle on a *recurved toothlet; indusium* cup-shaped, open at the
top.

In parts of the country, especially from Connecticut southward, the Hay-scented Fern is one of the
abundant plants. Though not essentially a rock-
loving plant, it rejoices in such rocky, upland
pastures as crown many of our lower mountain
ranges, "great stretches of grayish or sage-green
fields in which every bowlder and outcrop of rock
is marked by masses of the bright-green fronds
of *Dicksonia*, over which the air moves lazily, heavy
with the peculiar fragrance of this interesting fern."
Its singularly delicate, tapering, pale-green fronds,
curving gracefully in every direction, rank it among
our most beautiful and noticeable ferns. Often
along the roadsides it forms great masses of feathery foliage, tempting the weary pedestrian or bi-
cycler to fling himself upon a couch sufficiently
soft and luxurious in appearance to satisfy a syba-
rite. But I can testify that the Hay-scented Fern
does not make so good a bed as it promises.

Two years ago, during a memorably hot August,

114

PLATE XIV

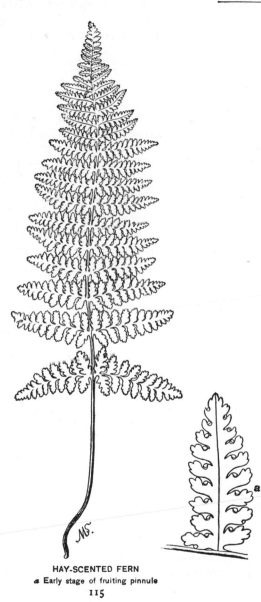

HAY-SCENTED FERN

a Early stage of fruiting pinnule

an afternoon drive over an unused mountain road
brought us to a picturesque spot where the clear
stream tumbled into a rock-paved basin, suggesting
so vividly the joy of

" —— the cool silver shock
Of the plunge in a pool's living water,"

that then and there we resolved soon to pitch our
tent upon its banks. In all respects it was not a
suitable camp site. There were no balsams or evergreens of any kind available for bedding in the
neighborhood, so when, a few days later, we had
taken up our quarters just above the rock-paved
pool, we went into our temporary back-yard where
the *Dicksonia* grew abundantly with its usual soft
and seductive appearance, and gathered great arm-
fuls for the night's rest. I must frankly own that I
never slept on so hard a bed. Since then I have
been more than ever inclined to believe that ferns
inhabit the earth chiefly for decorative ends. In
the present age they do not lend themselves as once
they did to medicinal purposes. Usually they are
without culinary value. So far as I know animals
refuse to eat them on account of their acrid juices.
And experience proves that when used as a bed
they do not

" —— medicine thee to that sweet sleep
Which thou owedst yesterday."

The Hay-scented Fern is very sensitive, withering with the early frosts. Sometimes in the fall it

bleaches almost white. Then its slender fronds seem like beautiful wraiths of their former selves.

The *Dicksonia*, as he always calls it, is Thoreau's favorite among the ferns. Its fronds are sweet-scented when crushed or in drying, and to their fragrance he was peculiarly sensitive:

"Going along this old Carlisle road . . . road where all wild things and fruits abound, where there are countless rocks to jar those who venture in wagons; road which leads to and through a great but not famous garden, zoölogical and botanical, at whose gate you never arrive—as I was going along there, I perceived the grateful scent of the Dicksonia fern now partly decayed. It reminds me of all up country, with its springy mountain-sides and unexhausted vigor. Is there any essence of Dicksonia fern, I wonder? Surely that giant, who my neighbor expects is to bound up the Alleghenies, will have his handkerchief scented with that. The sweet fragrance of decay! When I wade through by narrow cow-paths, it is as if I had strayed into an ancient and decayed herb garden. Nature perfumes her garments with this essence now especially. She gives it to those who go a-barberrying and on dark autumnal walks. The very scent of it, if you have a decayed frond in your chamber, will take you far up country in a twinkling. You would think you had gone after the cows there, or were lost on the mountains."

Again:

"Why can we not oftener refresh one another

with original thoughts? If the fragrance of the Dicksonia fern is so grateful and suggestive to us, how much more refreshing and encouraging, recreating, would be fresh and fragrant thoughts communicated to us from a man's experience? I want none of his pity nor sympathy in the common sense, but that he should emit and communicate to me his essential fragrance . . . going a-huckleberrying in the fields of thought, and enriching all the world with his vision and his joys."

In connection with this fern Thoreau indulges in one of those whimsical, enchanting disquisitions with the spirit of which you are in complete accord, even though you may seem to contradict the letter:

" It is only when we forget all our learning that we begin to know. I do not get nearer by a hair's-breadth to any natural object, so long as I presume that I have an introduction to it from some learned man. To conceive of it with a total apprehension, I must for the thousandth time approach it as something totally strange. If you would make acquaintance with the ferns, you must forget your botany. Not a single scientific term or distinction is the least to the purpose. You would fain perceive something, and you must approach the object totally unprejudiced. You must be aware that nothing is what you have taken it to be. In what book is this world and its beauty described? Who has plotted the steps toward the discovery of beauty? You must be in a different state from common. Your greatest success will be simply to perceive that such things are, and you will have no communication to make to the Royal Society. If it were required to know the position of the fruit-dots or the character of the indusium, nothing could be easier than to ascertain it ; but if it is required that you be affected by ferns, that they amount to anything, signify anything to you, that they be another sacred scripture and revelation to you, helping to redeem your life, this end is not so easily accomplished."

GROUP V

24. LADY FERN

Asplenium Filix-fœmina

A wood and roadside fern, growing in all parts of the country and presenting many varying forms. One to three feet high, with tufted, straw-colored, reddish, or brownish stalks.

Fronds.—Broadly lance-shaped, tapering toward the apex, twice-pinnate; *pinnæ* lance-shaped ; *pinnules* oblong-lanceolate, toothed or incised; *fruit-dots* short, curved ; *indusium* delicate, curved, sometimes shaped like a horseshoe.

The Lady Fern is found in all parts of the country. Sometimes it forms a part of the tangle of wild, graceful things which grow close to the roadside fence. Again, in company with the Silvery Spleenwort, the Evergreen Wood Fern and the Spinulose Shield Fern, forming perhaps a background for the brilliant scarlet clusters of the wild bergamot, it fringes the banks of some amber-colored brook which surprises us with its swift, noiseless flow as we stroll through the woods.

The earliest fronds uncurl in May. In June the

PLATE XV

LADY FERN

a Fruiting pinnule   *b* Portion of same

plant is very graceful and pleasing. When growing
in shaded places it is often conspicuous by reason
of its bright pink or reddish stalks, which contrast
effectively with the delicate green of the foliage.
But in later summer, judging by my own experience,
the Lady Fern loses much of its delicacy. Many
of its fronds become disfigured and present a rather
blotched and coarse appearance.

This seems strange in view of the fact that the
plant is called by Lowe, a well-known English writer,
the " Queen of Ferns," and that it is one of the few
ferns to which we find reference in literature. Scott
pays it the compliment, rarely bestowed upon ferns,
of mentioning it by name:

> " Where the copse wood is the greenest,
> Where the fountain glistens sheenest,
> Where the morning dew lies longest,
> There the Lady Fern grows strongest."

In English works devoted to ferns I find at least
two poems, more remarkable for enthusiasm than
for poetic inspiration, in its honor. I quote a portion
of the one which occurs in Miss Pratt's " Ferns of
Great Britain and Their Allies ":

> " But seek her not in early May,
>   For a Sibyl then she looks,
> With wrinkled fronds that seem to say,
>   ' Shut up are my wizard books ! '
> Then search for her in the summer woods,
>   Where rills keep moist the ground,
> Where Foxgloves from their spotted hoods,
>   Shake pilfering insects round ;

When up and clambering all about,
    The Traveller's Joy flings forth
Its snowy awns, that in and out
    Like feathers strew the earth :
Fair are the tufts of meadow-sweet
    That haply blossom nigh ;
Fair are the whirls of violet
    Prunella shows hard by ;
But nor by burn in wood, or vale,
    Grows anything so fair
As the plumy crest of emerald pale,
That waves in the wind, and soughs in the gale,
Of the Lady Fern, when the sunbeams turn
    To gold her delicate hair."

The other, which I give in full, on account of its quaintness, appeared in the *Botanical Looker-out* of Edwin Lees:

" When in splendor and beauty all nature is crown'd,
   The Fern is seen curling half hid in the ground,
   But of all the green brackens that rise by the burn,
   Commend me alone to the sweet Lady Fern.

" Polypodium indented stands stiff on the rock,
   With his sori exposed to the tempest's rough shock ;
   On the wide, chilly heath Aquilina stands stern,
   Not once to be named with the sweet Lady Fern.

" Filix-mas in a circle lifts up his green fronds
   And the Heath Fern delights by the bogs and the ponds ;
   Through their shadowy tufts though with pleasure I turn,
   The palm must still rest with the fair Lady Fern.

" By the fountain I see her just spring into sight,
   Her texture as frail as though shivering with fright ;
   To the water she shrinks—I can scarcely discern
   In the deep humid shadows the soft Lady Fern.

" Where the water is pouring forever she sits,
And beside her the Ouzel, the Kingfisher flits ;
There, supreme in her beauty, beside the full urn,
In the shade of the rock stands the tall Lady Fern.

" Noon burns up the mountain ; but here by the fall
The Lady Fern flourishes graceful and tall.
Hours speed as thoughts rise, without any concern,
And float like the spray gliding past the green Fern."

25. SILVERY SPLEENWORT

Asplenium thelypteroides (*A. acrostichoides*)

Entire frond

Canada to Alabama and westward, in rich woods.   One to three feet high.

Fronds. — Lance-shaped, tapering both ways from the middle, once-pinnate; *pinnæ* linear-lanceolate, deeply cut into obtuse segments; *fruit-dots* oblong; *indusium* silvery when young.

The Silvery Spleenwort grows in company with its kinsman, the Narrow-leaved Spleenwort, and also with many of the Aspidiums, such as the Spinulose Shield Fern, the Evergreen Wood Fern, the Christmas and Goldie's Fern.   I find it growing in large patches in the rich woods, often near water, either in boggy ground or on the very edge of the clear, brown brook. Sometimes it is difficult to detect a single fertile frond in a group of plants covering many square feet of ground.   This is probably owing

124

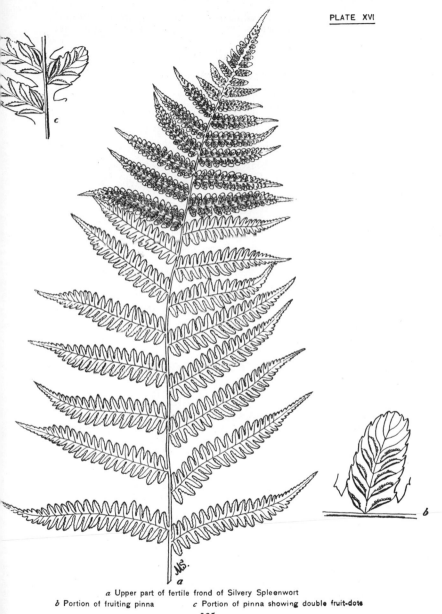

PLATE XVI

a Upper part of fertile frond of Silvery Spleenwort
b Portion of fruiting pinna   *c* Portion of pinna showing double fruit-dots

to the deeply shaded situations which it favors, as in sunny exposures I have noticed an abundance of fertile fronds.

Its color is a dull green, the silvery indusia on the lower surfaces of the pinnæ giving the plant its English title. Although usually its fronds are larger, their outline, tapering as it does both ways from the middle, somewhat suggests that of the New York Fern. It is readily identified, as the oblong or linear fruit-dots at once proclaim it a Spleenwort, and no other member of this tribe has fronds of the same shape.

Although it cannot be classed among the rare ferns, it is absent from many promising localities, and is associated in my mind with especially successful expeditions.

26. RUE SPLEENWORT. WALL RUE

Asplenium Ruta-muraria

A small rock fern, growing on limestone, Vermont to Michigan and southward. Four to seven inches long, with green, slender, tufted stalks.

Fronds.—Triangular-ovate, smooth, evergreen, twice or thrice-pinnate below; *pinnæ* cut into stalked pinnules; *fruit-dots* confluent at maturity, covering nearly the whole lower surface of pinnules; *indusium* delicate.

My first acquaintance with the little Rue Spleenwort in its own home dates back to the memorable day when we discovered the new station for the Hart's Tongue.

PLATE XVII

RUE SPLEENWORT

As I have already mentioned in my description of the Purple Cliff Brake, on a chance morning call I learned that twenty-five years before the Rue Spleenwort and the Purple Cliff Brake had been found on certain cliffs which overhung some neighboring falls.

On these very cliffs a quarter of a century later we found a few specimens of each plant. The tiny fronds of the Rue Spleenwort grew from small fissures in the cliffs, flattening themselves against their rocky background.

About a month later we returned to the spot for the purpose of securing photographs of the natural gallery where the plants grew. The seamed, overhanging rocks, the neighboring stream plunging nearly two hundred feet to the ravine below, the bold opposite cliffs showing here and there through their cloak of trees, and above and beyond the smiling upland pastures, the wood-crowned hills, and the haze-softened valley, had left a picture in the mind that we hoped to reproduce, however inadequately, by means of the camera.

This morning we had approached the cliffs from an opposite direction. In climbing a gradual ascent from the bed of the stream, we found a plant of the Rue Spleenwort which was more vigorous and thrifty than any we had previously seen. In the single tuft, about as large as the palm of one's hand, we counted forty-five green fronds. Their lower surfaces, in many cases, were covered with confluent fruit-dots. The plant had much the effect of a rather small spec-

imen of the Mountain Spleenwort. The short, broad
fronds were somewhat leathery, with only a few pinnæ. Considering its lack of size, the little cluster,
springing from the bare rock, made so definite and
interesting a picture that we tried to photograph it
as it grew. But after some time spent in striving to
secure a foothold for the tripod, and at the same
time for the photographer, we gave up the attempt
as hopeless.

In England the Rue Spleenwort is found growing
on old walls, specially on their northern sides, also
on church-towers, bridges, and ruins. It is said to
be difficult to cultivate.

Formerly this fern yielded a decoction which was
supposed to be beneficial in attacks of pleurisy and
of jaundice.

27. MOUNTAIN SPLEENWORT

Asplenium montanum

Connecticut and New York to Georgia. A small rock fern from two to eight inches long, with stalks brown at base.

Fronds. — Ovate-lanceolate in outline, somewhat leathery, cut into oblong pinnæ, the lower ones of which are cut again into more or less oblong, toothed divisions, the upper ones less and less divided; *rachis* green, broad, flat; *fruit-dots* linear, short; *indusium* thin, hidden at length by the sporangia, which mature in July.

With us this plant is decidedly rare. New York and Connecticut are given as its northern limits. I have found it only in one locality, in the neighborhood of a mountain lake in Ulster County, N. Y. Though growing here somewhat abundantly, the fern is so small that, unless your eyes are trained to search every cranny in the hope of some new find, you are not likely to notice it. Even with trained eyes you may readily fancy that the narrow chinks in the cliffs which rise sheerly from the lake are merely patched with moss. But when you have pulled your boat close under the shelving rocks,

PLATE XVIII

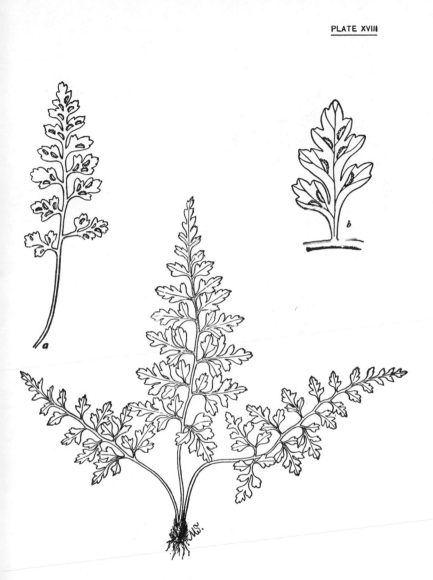

MOUNTAIN SPLEENWORT

a A fertile frond   *b* A pinna of fertile frond

and have secured a hold that enables you to stand
up and examine at leisure the suspicious patches,
your heart bounds with delight as you get a
near view of the fringe of blue-green, leathery
fronds which flatten themselves against the gray

Mountain Spleenwort

cliffs. Apparently
only the plants that
grow under specially
favorable conditions
are able to develop fronds that attain a length
of five or six inches. Only in what must have
been almost constant shadow, under the shelving
rocks, directly above the lake and refreshed
always by its moisture, did I find these really

attractive, thrifty-looking plants.   The specimens, which were located at some distance from the lake, growing in one instance on top of a mountain, again in the shaded crevices of a cliff, were tiny, indefinite-looking plants with nothing to recommend them to any eyes save those of the fern collector.   In every instance they grew from fissures in the rocks, rooting apparently in a mere pinch of earth, yet with such tenacity that it would have been very difficult to extract a plant unharmed.   In almost every case they were shielded much of the time from exposure to the sun.

The large plants in the immediate vicinity of the lake were noticeably bluish-green in color.

It is to be hoped that the few known haunts of the Mountain Spleenwort will be respected in order that this rare little plant may be preserved.

28. EBONY SPLEENWORT

Asplenium ebeneum (*A. platyneuron*)

Maine to Florida and westward, on rocks and hill-sides. Nine to eighteen inches high, with blackish and shining stalks.

Fronds.—Upright, narrowly oblanceolate, fertile fronds much the taller, once-pinnate; *pinnæ* usually alternate, oblong, finely toothed, the base auricled on the upper or on both sides; *fruit-dots* many, oblong, nearer midvein than margin; *indusium* silvery till maturity.

The slender fronds of the Ebony Spleenwort hold themselves with a sort of rigid grace which suggests a combination of delicacy and endurance.

Portion of fertile frond

It is an attractive plant with an elusiveness of habit which serves, perhaps, to increase its charm. Its range is from Maine to Florida and westward; it is said to prefer limestone soil, and my past experience has proved it a fairly common plant, yet so far this summer, in many expeditions in a part of the country rich in limestone, I have found only one specimen, while last year along the road-sides of Long Island I found its black-stemmed fronds standing erect and slim in crowded ranks under groups of red cedars. In other years it has abounded in localities of a different character,

Fertile pinna magnified

sometimes following its little relative, the Maiden-hair Spleenwort, into moist ravines or along

134

PLATE XIX

EBONY SPLEENWORT

135

the shelves of shaded rocks, again climbing exposed hill-sides, where its fresh beauty is always a surprise.

The fronds of the Ebony Spleenwort usually face the sun, even if so doing necessitates the twisting of its stalk.

29. MAIDENHAIR SPLEENWORT

Asplenium Trichomanes

Almost throughout North America.   A small rock fern, four to twelve inches long, with purplish-brown and shining, thread-like stalks.

Fronds.—Linear in outline, somewhat rigid, once-pinnate; *pinnæ* roundish or oval, unequal-sided, attached to rachis by a narrow point, entire or toothed; *fruit-dots* short, oblong, narrowed at the ends, three to six on each side of the midrib; *sporangia* dark-brown when ripe; *indusium* delicate.

In childhood the delicate little fronds and dark, glistening, thread-like stalks of the Maidenhair Spleenwort seemed to me a token of the mysterious,

Fertile pinnæ

ecstatic presence of the deeper woods, of woods where dark hemlocks arched across the rock-broken stream, where the spongy ground was carpeted with low, nameless plants with white-veined or shining leaves and coral-like berries, where precious red-cupped mosses covered the fallen tree-trunks and strange birds sang unknown songs.

Perhaps because in those days it was a rare plant

to be met with on rare occasions, in a spirit of breathless exultation, I almost begrudge finding it now on shaded cliffs close to the highway.

Certainly it seems lovelier when it holds itself somewhat aloof from the beaten paths. One of its favorite haunts is a mossy cliff which forms part of a ravine of singular beauty. Along the base of this cliff foams a rushing stream on its way to the valley. Overhead stretch branches of hemlock, cedar, and basswood.

Maidenhair Spleenwort

On the broader shelves the mountain maple, the silver birch, and the hobble-bush secure a precarious foothold. Below rare sunbeams bring out rich patches of color on the smooth, muscular trunks of the beeches. Close to the water, perhaps, wheel a pair of spotted sand-pipers, now

lighting on the rocks in order to secure some in-
sect, now tilting backward and forward with the

comical motion peculiar to them,
now gliding swiftly along the
pebbly shore till their brown and
gray and white coats are lost in
the brown and gray and white of

Lower pinnæ   shore, rock, and water.

In such a retreat as this ravine the Maidenhair
Spleenwort seems peculiarly at home.   Its tufted
fronds have a fresh greenness that
is a delight to the eye as they spring
from little pockets or crannies too
shallow, we would suppose, for the
necessary moisture and nourishment.
Its near companions are the Walking Fern, whose tapering, leaf-like,
blue-green fronds leap along the   Upper pinnæ

shelving ledge above, and the Bulblet Bladder Fern,
which seems to gush from every crevice of the cliff.

30. GREEN SPLEENWORT

Asplenium viride

Northern New England, west and northward, on shaded rocks.
A few inches to nearly a foot long, with tufted stalks, brownish
below, green above.

Fronds.—Linear-lanceolate, once-pinnate, pale green ; *pinnæ*
ovate, toothed, midvein indistinct and forking ; *fruit-dots* oblong ;
indusium straight or curved.

The Green Spleenwort in general appearance
resembles the Maidenhair Spleenwort.   Perhaps

138

PLATE XX

GREEN SPLEENWORT

139

its most distinguishing feature is its stalk, which, though brown below, becomes green above, while that of its little relative is dark and shining throughout.   Its discovery on Mt. Mansfield, Vt., by Mr. Pringle gave it a place in the flora of the United

States, as is shown in the following passage from Mr Pringle's address before the Vermont Botanical Club:

"On this first visit to Mt. Mansfield my work was restricted to the crest of the great mountain.   About the cool and shaded cliffs in front of the Summit House were then first brought to my view *Aspidium fragrans* . . . and

Fertile pinnæ

Asplenium viride, . . . for I was still on my fern hunt.   The finding of the former added a species to the Vermont catalogue; the latter was an addition to the flora of the United States.   Such little discoveries gave joy to the young collector."

31. SCOTT'S SPLEENWORT

Asplenium ebenoides

Connecticut to the Mississippi and southward to Alabama, on limestone.   Four to twelve inches long, with blackish and shining stalks.

Fronds.—Lanceolate, tapering to a long, narrow apex, generally pinnate below, pinnatifid above; *fruit-dots* straight or slightly curved; *indusium* narrow.

PLATE XXI

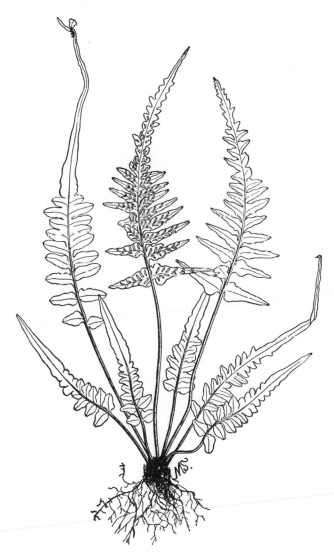

SCOTT'S SPLEENWORT

141

The known stations of this curious little plant are usually in the immediate neighborhood of the Walking Leaf and the Ebony Spleenwort, of which ferns it is supposed to be a hybrid. The long, narrow apex occasionally forming a new plant, and the irregular fruit-dots remind one of the Walking Leaf, while the lustrous black stalk, the free veins, and the pinnate portions of the fronds suggest the Ebony Spleenwort.

Scott's Spleenwort matures in August. It is rare and local, except in Alabama. The fact, however, that it has been discovered in widely distant localities east of the Mississippi should lend excitement to fern expeditions in any of our limestone neighborhoods where we see its chosen associates, the Walking Leaf and the Ebony Spleenwort. To find a new station for this interesting little fern, even if it consisted of one or two plants only, as is said to have been the case at Canaan, Conn., would well repay the fatigue of the longest tramp.

32. PINNATIFID SPLEENWORT

Asplenium pinnatifidum

New Jersey and Pennsylvania to Illinois, and southward to Alabama and Arkansas, on rocks. Four to fourteen inches long, with polished stalks, blackish below, green above, when young somewhat chaffy below.

Fronds.—Broadly lance-shaped, tapering to a long, slender point, pinnatifid or pinnate below ; *pinnæ* rounded or the lowest tapering to a point , *fruit-dots* straight or somewhat curved ; *indusium* straight or curved.

142

PLATE XXII

PINNATIFID SPLEENWORT

This plant resembles the Walking Leaf to such an extent that formerly it was not considered a separate species. The long, slender apex of its frond, which, it is said, sometimes takes root, as in the Walking Leaf, gave ground for its confusion with that fern. But the tapering apex of the frond of the Pinnàtifid Spleenwort is not so long and the veins of the frond are free.

The Pinnatifid Spleenwort grows on rocks. Its usual companions are the Mountain Spleenwort and the Maidenhair Spleenwort. Williamson tells us that, though it is quite common in Kentucky, he has never found a frond which rooted at the apex. Eaton, however, speaks of "one or two instances of a slight enlargement of the apex, as if there were an attempt to form a proliferous bud."

33. BRADLEY'S SPLEENWORT

Asplenium Bradleyi

New York to Georgia and Alabama, westward to Arkansas, on rocks preferring limestone. Six to ten inches long, with slender, chestnut-brown stalks.

Fronds.—Oblong-lanceolate or oblong, tapering to a point, pinnate; *pinnæ* oblong-ovate, lobed or pinnatifid; *fruit-dots* short, near the midrib; *indusium* delicate.

To my knowledge the only place in the northeastern States where this rare and local species has been collected is near Newburg, N. Y., where Dr. Eaton found a plant growing on lime rock in 1864.

PLATE XXIII

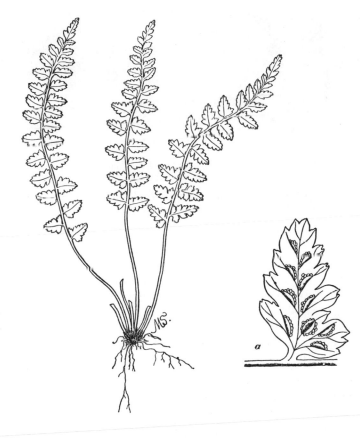

BRADLEY'S SPLEENWORT

a Fertile pinna

145

34. WALKING FERN.
WALKING LEAF

Camptosorus rhizophyllus

Canada to North Carolina and westward, on shaded rocks, preferring limestone. Four to eighteen inches long, with light-green stalks.

Fronds.—Simple, lanceolate, long-tapering toward the apex, usually heart-shaped at base, the apex often rooting and forming a new plant ; *fruit-dots* oblong or linear, irregularly scattered on the lower surface of the frond ; *indusium* thin.

To its unusual and suggestive title this plant undoubtedly owes much of the interest which it seems to arouse in the minds of those who do not profess to be fern-lovers. A friend tells me that as a child, eagerly on the lookout for this apparently active little plant, he was so much influenced by its title that he thought it might be advantageous to secure a butterfly-net as an aid in its capture. I find that older people as well are tempted to unwonted energy if promised a glimpse of the Walking Fern. Then, too, the scarcity of the plant in many localities, or, indeed, its entire absence from certain parts of the country, gives it a reputation for rarity which is one of the most certain roads to fame.

For many years I was unable to track it to any of its haunts. During a summer spent in Rensselaer County, N. Y., the Walking Leaf was the object of various expeditions. I recall one drive of twenty-five miles devoted to hunting up a rumored station. At the end of the day, which turned out cold and rainy, and fruitless so far as its special object was concerned, I felt inclined to believe that the plant had justified its title and had walked out of the neighborhood. Yet, after all, no such expedition, even with wind and weather against one, as in this case, is really fruitless. The sharp watch along the roadside, the many little expeditions into inviting

Portion of fertile frond

pastures, up promising cliffs, over moss-grown bowlders, down to the rocky border of the brook, are sure to result in discoveries of value or in moments of delight. A flower yet unnamed, a butterfly beautiful as a gem, an unfamiliar bird-song traced to its source, a new, suggestive outlook over the well-known valley, and, later, "a sleep pleasant with all the influences of long hours in the open air"—any or all of these results may be ours, and go to make the day count.

Finally, one September afternoon, shortly before leaving the neighborhood, we resolved upon a last search, in quite a new direction.   Several miles from home, at a fork in the road, standing in a partially wooded pasture, we noticed just such a large, shaded rock, with mossy ledges, as had filled us with vain hopes many times.   J. suggested a closer examination, which I discouraged, remembering previous disappointments.   But something in the look of the great bowlder provoked his curiosity, so over the fence and up the ledges he scrambled.   Almost his first resting-place was a projecting shelf which was carpeted with a mat of bluish-green foliage.   It needed only a moment's investigation to identify the leathery, tapering fronds of the Walking Fern.   No one who has not spent hours in some such search as this can sympathize with the delight of those moments.   We fairly gloated over the quaint little plants, following with our fingers the slender tips of the fronds till they rooted in the moss, starting another generation on its life journey, and earning for itself the title of Walking Leaf or Walking Fern.

Although since then I have found the Walking Leaf frequently, and in great abundance, I do not remember ever to have seen it make so fine a display. The plants were unusually large and vigorous, and the aspect of the matted tufts was uncommonly luxuriant.   To be sure, some allowance must be made for the glamour of a first meeting.

The Walking Leaf grows usually on limestone

148

rocks, though it has been found on sandstone, shale, and conglomerate as well.   I have also seen it on the stumps of decaying trees near limestone cliffs in Central New York, where it is a common plant, creeping along the shaded, mossy ledges above star-like tufts of the Maidenhair Spleenwort and fragile clusters of the Slender Cliff Brake, venturing to the brook's edge with sprays of the Bulblet Bladder Fern, and climbing the turreted summits of the hills close to the Purple Cliff Brake.

Although without the grace of the Maidenhair, the delicacy of certain of the Spleenworts, or the stately beauty of the Shield Ferns, the oddity and sturdiness of this little plant are bound to make it a favorite everywhere.

Occasionally a plant is found which will keep up its connection with two or three generations; that is, a frond will root at the apex, forming a new plant (the second generation). This will also send out a rooting frond which gives birth to a new plant (the third generation) before the two first fronds have decayed at their tips so as to sever the connection.

At times forking fronds are found, these forks also rooting occasionally at their tips.

35. HART'S TONGUE

Scolopendrium vulgare (S. scolopendrium)

Shaded ravines under limestone cliffs in Central New York and near South Pittsburg, Tenn. A few inches to nearly two feet long, with stalks which are chaffy below and sometimes to the base of the leaf.

Fronds.—Narrowly oblong, undivided, from a somewhat heart-shaped base, bright-green ; *fruit-dots* linear, elongated, a row on either side of the midrib and at right angles to it ; *indusium* appearing to be double.

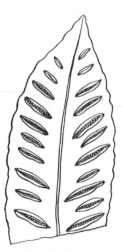

Tip of fertile frond

When Gray describes a fern as " very rare " and Dr. Britton limits it to two small stations in neighboring counties in the whole northern United States, the fern lover looks forward with a sense of eager anticipation to seeing it for the first time.

During a week spent at Cazenovia, N. Y., a few years ago, I learned that the rare Hart's Tongue grew at Chittenango Falls, only four miles away. But my time was limited, and on a single brief visit to the picturesque spot where the broad Chittenango stream dashes over cliffs one hundred and fifty feet high, losing itself in the wild, wooded glen below on its journey to the distant valley, I did little more than revel in the beauty of the foaming mass which for many days " haunted me like a pas-

sion." I saw no signs of the plant which has done almost as much as "the sounding cataract" to make the spot famous.

The combined recollection of the beautiful falls and the for me undiscovered fern, joined to the fact that Madison and the adjoining Onondaga County are favorite hunting grounds for the fern lover on account of the many species which they harbor, drew us to Cazenovia for the summer two years later.

Guided by the explicit directions of Mr. J. H. Ten Eyck Burr, a fern enthusiast who is always ready to share with others, of whose good faith he is assured, his enjoyment of the hiding-places of his favorites, we found at last the Hart's Tongue in its own home.

Hart's Tongue

If Mr. Burr's kindness in sending me some fine pressed specimens, and the illustrations I had seen in various books, had not already made me familiar with the general look of the plant, the long, undivided, tongue-like fronds, so different from one's preconceived notion of a fern, would have been a great surprise. Even now, although I have visited many times its hidden retreats, and have noted with delight every detail of its glossy, vigorous growth, it seems to me always as rare and unusual as it did the first day I found it.

At Chittenango Falls the Hart's Tongue grows a few yards from the base of bold, overhanging limestone cliffs, the tops of which are fringed by pendent roots of the red cedar. Nearly always it is caught beneath moss-grown fragments of the fallen limestone, the bright-green, undulating, glossy leaves either standing almost erect (curving outward slightly above) or else falling over toward the slope of the land so as to present a nearly prostrate appearance. At times these fronds are very numerous, as many as fifty to a plant, forming great clumps of foliage. Again we find a plant with only half a dozen or even fewer green fronds. At maturity the linear, bright-brown fruit-dots, a row on either side the midrib, are conspicuous on the lower surfaces of the fronds.

This haunt of the Hart's Tongue is shaded by a growth of tall basswoods and maples, of sturdy oaks and hemlocks. The neighboring cliffs are draped with the slender fronds of the Bulblet Bladder Fern. On every side rise the tall crowns of the omnipresent Evergreen Wood Fern. Lower down, close to the rushing stream which we see mistily through the green branches, its roar always in our ears, grow the Walking Leaf and the Maidenhair. The little Polypody climbs over the rocks and perches contentedly on the spreading roots of trees, while a few fragile plants of the Slender Cliff Brake, something of a rarity in these parts, are fastened to the mossy ledges.

The other published northern station of the Hart's Tongue is at Jamesville, some fifteen miles from Chittenango Falls, near a small sheet of water known commonly as Green Pond, christened botanically Scolopendrium Lake. Here also it grows among the talus at the foot of limestone cliffs. The plants which I found in this locality were less luxuriant than those at Chittenango Falls. They grow in more exposed, less shaded spots.

Scolopendrium Lake has become somewhat famous in the world of fern students by reason of Mr. Underwood's claim that in its immediate vicinity, within a radius of fifty rods from the water's edge (the lake being a mere pond), grow twenty-seven different kinds of ferns, while within a circle whose diameter is not over three miles thirty-four species have been found. During this one day we gave to the neighborhood, we could not hope to find so great a number, the result, perhaps, of many days' investigation, and were forced to content ourselves with the twenty-one species we did find. In

153

his list Mr. Underwood marks the Purple Cliff
Brake as found but once, so I judge he did not discover the station on the turreted cliffs close by
where it grows in extravagant profusion, producing
fronds not only much longer and finer than I had
seen elsewhere, but superior to those pictured in
the illustrated books.

During the same summer, on an expedition to
Perryville Falls, which we had planned for the
express purpose of finding the Rue Spleenwort and
the Purple Cliff Brake, a new station was discovered for the Hart's Tongue.   To Miss Murray Ledyard, of Cazenovia, belongs the honor of finding the
first plants in this locality.   We had been successful in the original object of our journey, and had
crossed the stream in order to examine the opposite cliffs.   J. and I, curious to study the wet wall
of rock close to the sheer white veil of water, which
fell more than one hundred feet, finally secured
an unsubstantial foothold among graceful tufts of
the greenish, lily-like flowers, which ought to receive a more homely and appropriate title than
Zygadenus elegans.   Having satisfied ourselves that
the mossy crevices harbored no plants of the Slender Cliff Brake, now the immediate object of our
search, we followed the natural path beneath the
overhanging rock and above the sheer descent to
the ravine, examining the cliffs as we cautiously
picked our way.   Miss Ledyard had remained below, and suddenly we heard her give a triumphant
shout, followed by the joyful announcement that

she had found the Hart's Tongue. The station
being previously quite unknown, this was a most
interesting discovery. On entering the ravine we
had discussed its possibility, but I had fancied that
any hope of it would be unfounded, as I supposed
the ground had been thoroughly canvassed by the
many botanists who had visited the neighborhood.

The plants were still young, but large and vigorous, growing in a partial opening among the basswoods, maples, and beeches, on a steep slope covered with fragments of limestone, some thirty or
forty feet from the base of the cliffs. We must
have found from twenty to thirty plants within a
radius of as many feet.

Unfortunately, as it turned out, the discovery
found its way to the columns of the local paper,
and on our return to the station, some weeks later
our eager expectation of seeing the young plants
in the splendor of maturity was crushed by finding that the spot had been ruthlessly invaded and
a number of the finest plants had disappeared. Before long it will be necessary for botanists to form a
secret society, with vows of silence as to fern localities and some sort of lynch law for the punishment
of vandals.

This fern, so rare with us, is a common plant in
Europe, its fronds attaining at times a length of two
or three feet. In Ireland and the Channel Islands
it is especially abundant. In Devonshire, England,
it is described as growing " on the tops and at the
sides of walls ; hanging from old ruins . . . drop-

ping down its long, green fronds into the cool
and limpid water of roadside wells hewn out of the
rock ; often exposed to the full blaze of the sun,
but always in such cases dwindled down to a tiny
size " (" The Fern Paradise ").

The Hart's Tongue has been known as the Cater-
pillar Fern and the Seaweed Fern.

36. VIRGINIA CHAIN FERN

Woodwardia Virginica

Swampy places, often in deep water, from Maine to Florida. Two
to more than three feet high.

Fronds.—Once-pinnate ; *pinnæ* pinnatifid, with oblong segments ; *fruit-dots* oblong, in chain-like rows along the midrib
both of the pinnæ and of the lobes, confluent when ripe ; *indusium*
fixed by its outer margin, opening on the side next the midrib.

Emerging from the shade and silence of a little
wood upon the rolling downs where one has
glimpses of the blue bay, our attention is attracted
by a tall fern beside the path, growing among a
tangle of shrubs and vines. It does not grow in
symmetrical crowns or tufts like an *Osmunda*, but
its fronds are almost as handsome, the divisions
being wider apart and more scattered. Turning
over two or three of the rather glossy fronds, we
find a rusty-backed, fertile frond, covered on one
side with the regular chain-like rows of fruit-dots
which make its name of Chain Fern seem very
appropriate and descriptive.

156

PLATE XXIV

UPPER PART OF FROND OF VIRGINIA CHAIN FERN
a Portion of fertile pinna   *b* Tip of fertile pinna

157

In the low, damp ground near the coast one may
expect to find this fern ; its haunts, where the narrow path winds between tall masses of sweet-pepper
bush and wet meadows where pogonia and calopo-
gon delight us in July, and the white-fringed orchids
may be found in later summer, are among the most
beautiful of the many beautiful kinds of country
that the fern and flower lover knows, to which his
feet stray inevitably in the season of green things,
and which are the solace of his "inward eye" when
that season is past.

GROUP VI

FERTILE AND STERILE FRONDS LEAF-LIKE AND USUALLY SIMILAR, FRUIT-DOTS ROUND

37. NEW YORK FERN

Aspidium Noveboracense (*Dryopteris Noveboracensis*)

Newfoundland to South Carolina, in woods and open meadows. One to more than two feet high, with stalks shorter than the fronds.

Fronds. — Lance-shaped, tapering both ways from the middle pinnate ; *pinnæ* lance-shaped, the lowest pairs shorter and deflexed, divided into flat, oblong lobes which are not reflexed over the fruit-dots ; *fruit-dots* round, distinct, near the margin ; *indusium* minute.

At times the pale-green fronds of the New York Fern throng to the roadside, which is flanked by a tangled thicket of Osmundas, wild roses, and elder bushes.

Again, they stay quietly at home in the open marsh or in the shadow of the hemlocks and cedars, where they have fragrant pyrola and pipsissewa for company, and where the long, melancholy note of the peewee breaks the silence.

This plant is easily distinguished from the Marsh Fern by the noticeable tapering at both ends of its frond, and by the flat instead of reflexed margins to the lobes of the fertile pinnæ.

38. MARSH FERN

Aspidium Thelypteris (*Dryopteris Thelypteris*)

New Brunswick to Florida, in wet woods and swamps.   One to
nearly three feet high.

Fronds. — Lance-shaped, slightly downy, once-pinnate, fertile fronds longer-stalked than the sterile; *pinnæ,* the lower ones hardly smaller than the others, cut into oblong, entire lobes, which are obtuse in the sterile fronds, but appear acute in the fertile ones from the strongly revolute margins; veins once or twice forked; *fruit-dots* small, round, half-way between midvein and margin, or nearer margin, soon confluent; *indusium* small.

In our wet woods and open swamps, and occasionally in dry pastures, the erect, fresh-green fronds of the Marsh Fern grow abundantly.   The lowest pinnæ are set so high on the long slender stem as to give the fern the appearance of trying to keep dry, daintily holding its skirts out of the mud as it were.

The plant's range is wide.   As I pick my way through marshy inland woods, using as bridges the fallen trunks and interlacing roots of trees, its bright fronds standing nearly three feet high, crowd about me.   Close by, securing, like myself, a firmer foothold by the aid of the trees' roots, I notice the flat,

PLATE XXV

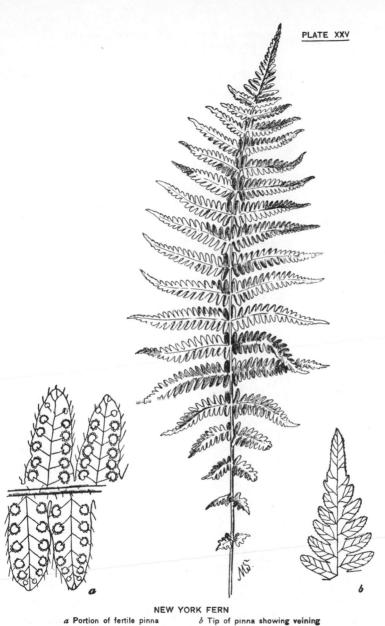

NEW YORK FERN

a Portion of fertile pinna   *b* Tip of pinna showing veining

mottled green and white rosettes and the slender wands of flowers of the rattlesnake orchid. In the open swamps beyond the fern's companion is another orchid, the ladies' tresses, with braided spikes of white, and in this case deliciously fragrant flowers.

In open marshes near the sea I find this plant associating itself with the violet-scented adder's mouth, with glistening sundew, and with gaudy Turk's-cap lilies. From the New

York Fern it may be distinguished easily by the somewhat abrupt

Marsh Fern

PLATE XXVI

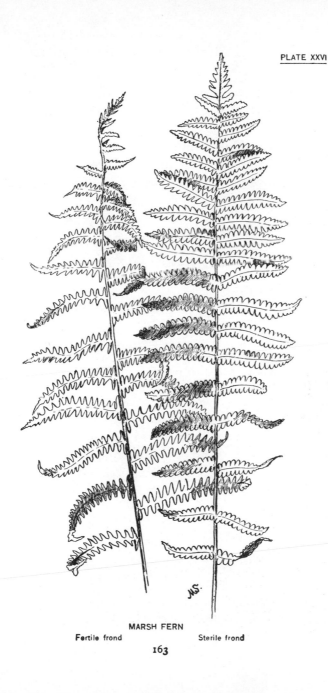

MARSH FERN

Fertile frond   Sterile frond

instead of tapering base of the frond, by the strongly revolute margins of the fertile frond, and by its long stalk.

From the Massachusetts Fern it may be distinguished by its forked veins, the less revolute margins of the fertile frond, and by its thicker texture and deeper green.

39. MASSACHUSETTS FERN

Aspidium simulatum (Dryopteris simulata)

New Hampshire to the Indian Territory, in wooded swamps. One to more than three feet high.

Fronds.—Oblong-lance-shaped, little or not at all narrowed at the base, rather thin, pinnate ; *pinnæ* lance-shaped, cut into oblong, obtuse segments, which are slightly reflexed in the fertile fronds, veins not forked ; *fruit-dots* rather large, somewhat distant ; *indusium* " withering-persistent."

This species closely resembles the Marsh Fern. The less revolute margins of the fertile frond, the simple veins, its thinner texture, and its more distant fruit-dots aid in its identification. It is found in woodland swamps from New Hampshire to the Indian Territory.

PLATE XXVII

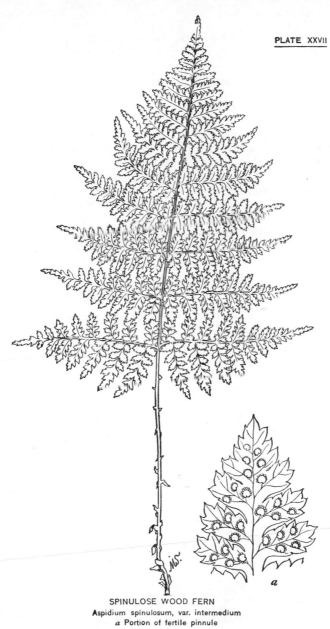

SPINULOSE WOOD FERN
Aspidium spinulosum, var. intermedium
a Portion of fertile pinnule

165

40. SPINULOSE WOOD FERN

Aspidium spinulosum (*Dryopteris spinulosa*)

Newfoundland to Kentucky. The common European type, rare in North America. One to two and a half feet high, with stalks having a few pale-brown deciduous scales.

Fronds.—Lance-ovate, twice-pinnate; *pinnæ* oblique to the rachis, elongated-triangular, the lower ones broadly triangular; *pinnules* oblique to the midrib, connected by a narrow wing, cut into thorny-toothed segments; *fruit-dots* round; *indusium* smooth, without marginal glands, soon withering.

To my knowledge I have only seen this fern in the herbarium, it being rare in this country. It is found, I have been told, chiefly toward the tops of mountains. Its pinnæ are noticeably ascending.

Var. intermedium (*D. spinulosa intermedia*)

Labrador to North Carolina, in woods almost everywhere. Usually large, with somewhat chaffy stalks, having brown, dark-centred scales.

Fronds.—Oblong-ovate, 2-3 pinnate; *pinnæ* oblong-lance-shaped, spreading, rather distant, the lowest unequally triangular, the pinnules on the lower side longer than those on the upper side; *pinnules* ovate-oblong, spreading, with oblong lobes thorny-toothed at the apex; *fruit-dots* round; *indusium* delicate, beset with tiny stalked glands.

This is the form of the species that abounds in our woods. Perhaps no one plant does more for their beauty than this stately fern, whose rich-green, outward-curving fronds spring in circles from fallen trees and decaying stumps as well as from the ground.

The plant varies greatly in height, breadth, and

PLATE XXVIII

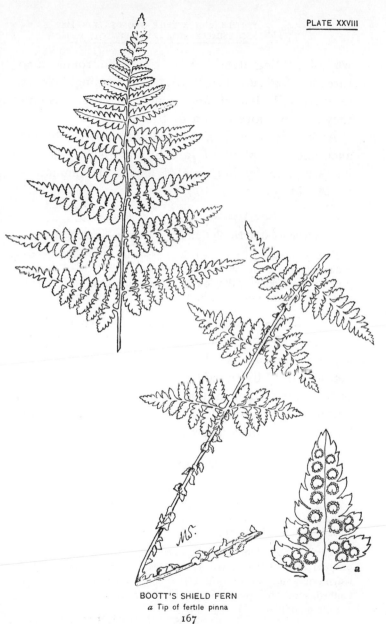

BOOTT'S SHIELD FERN
a Tip of fertile pinna
167

way of holding itself.   Sometimes the fronds stand
three feet high, and are broad and spreading.   Again,
they are tall, slender, and somewhat erect.   Again,
they are not more than a foot high.

At its best it grows with almost tropical luxuriance and is a plant of rare beauty, its fronds having a certain featheriness of aspect uncommon in
the Aspidiums.

Var. dilatatum (D. spinulosa dilatata)

Newfoundland to North Carolina, chiefly in the mountains.

Fronds.—Usually large, broader at base than in either of the preceding species, ovate or triangular-ovate, oftenest thrice-pinnate;
pinnules lance-oblong, the lowest often much elongated; *fruit-
dots* round; *indusium* smooth.

This form of the Spinulose Wood Fern is distinguished chiefly by its broader fronds and by the
smooth indusia.   As these indusia can be seen satisfactorily only by the aid of a magnifying-glass, there
is frequently some difficulty in distinguishing this
variety.   Occasionally it occurs in a dwarf state,
fruiting when only a few inches high.

41. BOOTT'S SHIELD FERN

Aspidium Boottii (Dryopteris Boottii)

Nova Scotia to Maryland, about ponds and in wet places.
One and a half to more than three feet high, with somewhat chaffy
stalks which have pale-brown scales.

Fronds.—Long lance-shaped, somewhat narrowed at base, nearly
or quite twice-pinnate; *pinnæ*, the lowest triangular-ovate, upper
longer and narrower; *pinnules* oblong-ovate, sharply thorny-
toothed, somewhat pinnatifid below; *fruit-dots* round; *indusium*
slightly glandular.

PLATE XXIX

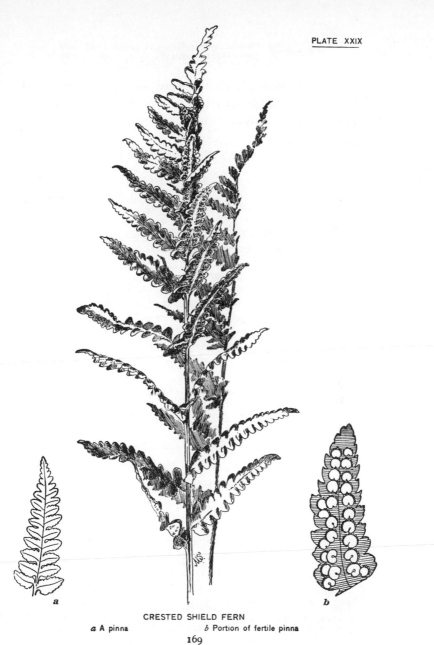

CRESTED SHIELD FERN

a A pinna   *b* Portion of fertile pinna

169

Boott's Shield Fern is found in moist woods and near ponds. It is distinguished by its long, narrow fronds and minutely glandular indusium.

42. CRESTED SHIELD FERN

Aspidium cristatum (*Dryopteris cristata*)

Newfoundland to Kentucky, in swamps. One to more than three feet high, with stalks which are chaffy, especially below, and which have light-brown scales, stalks of sterile fronds much shorter than those of fertile fronds.

Fronds.—Linear-oblong or lance-shaped, nearly twice-pinnate, fertile ones taller and longer stalked than the sterile; *pinnæ* (of the fertile frond, turning their faces toward the apex of the frond) rather short, lance-shaped or triangular-oblong, deeply impressed with veins, cut deeply into oblong, obtuse, finely toothed divisions; *fruit-dots* large, round, half-way between midvein and margin; *indusium* large, flat.

In wet woods, growing either from the ground or from the trunks of fallen trees, and also in open meadows, we notice the tall, slender, dark-green, somewhat lustrous fronds of the Crested Shield Fern, usually distinguished easily from its kinsmen by the noticeably upward-turning pinnæ of the fertile fronds, and by the deep impression made by the veins on their upper surfaces.

The sterile fronds are much shorter than the fertile ones. They are evergreen, lasting through the winter after the fertile fronds have perished.

Near the Crested Shield Fern we find often many of its kinsmen, broad, feathery fronds of the Spinulose Wood Fern, more slender ones of Boott's Shield

PLATE XXX

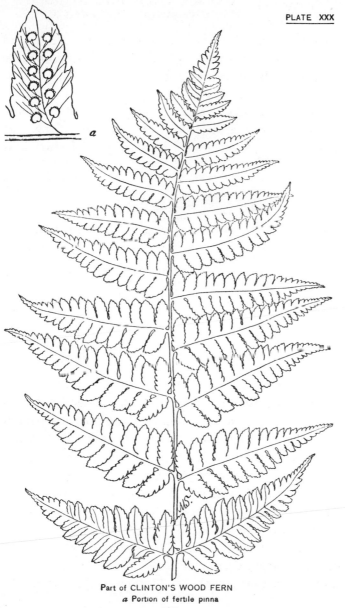

Part of CLINTON'S WOOD FERN
a Portion of fertile pinna

171

Fern, great tufts made by the magnificent bright-
green fronds of Goldie's Fern, symmetrical circles
of vigorous Evergreen Wood Fern, and shining clusters of the Christmas Fern.   All these plants, belonging to the one tribe, seek the same moist, shaded
retreats, and form a group of singular beauty and
vigor.

43. CLINTON'S WOOD FERN

*Aspidium cristatum, var. Clintonianum (Dryopteris cristata Clinto-
niana)*

Maine to New Jersey and Pennsylvania, in swampy woods.   Two
and a half to four feet high.

Fronds.—Larger in every way than those of the Crested Shield
Fern, nearly twice-pinnate; *pinnæ broadest at base*, cut into from
eight to sixteen pairs of linear-oblong, obtuse, obscurely toothed divisions; *fruit-dots* large, round, near the midvein; *indusium* orbicular, smooth.

This is a much larger and more showy plant than
the Crested Shield Fern.   Its tall, broad, hardy-
looking fronds are found in our moist woods.   While
not rare it is exclusive in its habits, and cannot be
classed with such every-day finds as its kinsmen,
the Marsh, Spinulose, Evergreen, and Christmas
Ferns.

PLATE XXXI

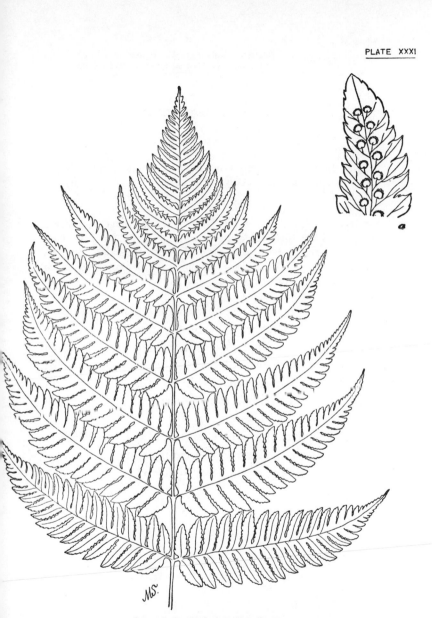

Part of fertile frond of Goldie's Fern
a Portion of a fertile pinna

44. GOLDIE'S FERN

Aspidium Goldianum (*Dryopteris Goldieana*)

New Brunswick to North Carolina and Tennessee, in rich woods. Two to more than four feet high, with stalks which are chaffy near the base.

Fronds.—Broadly ovate, the early sterile ones much broader in proportion and smaller, usually a foot or more wide, once-pinnate; *pinnæ* pinnatifid; *broadest in the middle* (the distinction from Clinton's Wood Fern), the divisions, about twenty pairs, oblong-linear, slightly toothed; *fruit-dots* very near the midvein; *indusium* very large, orbicular.

In the golden twilight of the deeper woods this stately plant unfurls its tall, broad, bright - green fronds, studded on their backs with the round fruit-dots which are so noticeable in this *Aspidium*, adding much to their attractiveness by the suggestion of fertility.

This plant ranks with the Osmundas and with the Ostrich Fern in size and vigorous beauty. Its retiring habits give it a reputation for rarity or at least for exclusiveness.

PLATE XXXII

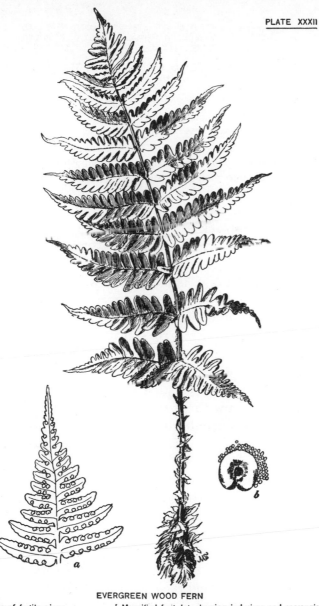

EVERGREEN WOOD FERN

a Tip of fertile pinna   *b* Magnified fruit-dot, showing indusium and sporangia

175

45. EVERGREEN WOOD FERN. MARGINAL SHIELD FERN

Aspidium marginale (*Dryopteris marginalis*)

Canada to Alabama, in rocky woods. A few inches to three feet high, with more or less chaffy stalks having shining scales.

Fronds.—Ovate-oblong, smooth, thick, somewhat leathery, once or twice-pinnate; *pinnæ* lance-shaped or triangular-ovate, tapering at the end, cut into pinnules; *pinnules* oblong, entire, or toothed; *fruit-dots* large, round, close to the margin; *indusium* large, convex, persistent.

Above the black leaf-mould in our rocky northern woods rise the firm, graceful crowns formed by the blue-green fronds of the Evergreen Wood Fern. The plant bears a family likeness to the Crested Shield Fern, but its conspicuously marginal fruit-dots identify it at sight.

It is interesting to read that it comes "nearer being a tree-fern than any other of our species, the caudex covered by the bases of fronds of previous seasons, sometimes resting on bare rocks for four or five inches without roots or fronds" (see Eaton, p. 70). This peculiarity in the plant's growth is often striking and certainly suggests the tree-ferns of the green-house.

Frequently in this species I notice what is more or less common to nearly all ferns, the exquisite contrast in the different shades of green worn by the younger and older fronds and the charming effect produced when the deep green of the centre of a frond shades away in the most delicate manner toward its apex and the tips of its pinnules.

As its English title signifies, the Evergreen Wood

Fern flourishes throughout the winter. In one of
the October entries in his journal, Thoreau records
his satisfaction in the endurance of the hardy ferns:
" Now they are conspicuous amid the withered
leaves. You are inclined to approach and raise each
frond in succession, moist, trembling, fragile greenness. They linger thus in all moist, clammy swamps
under the bare maples and grapevines and witch
hazels, and about each trickling spring that is half
choked with fallen leaves. What means this persistent vitality? Why were these spared when the
brakes and osmundas were stricken down? They
stay as if to keep up the spirits of the cold-blooded
frogs which have not yet gone into the mud, that
the summer may die with decent and graceful mod-
eration. Is not the water of the spring improved
by their presence? They fall back and droop here
and there like the plumes of departing summer, of
the departing year. Even in them I feel an argu-
ment for immortality. Death is so far from being
universal. The same destroyer does not destroy
all. How valuable they are, with the lycopodiums,
for cheerfulness. Greenness at the end of the year,
after the fall of the leaf, a hale old age. To my eye
they are tall and noble as palm-groves, and always
some forest nobleness seems to have its haunt under
their umbrage. All that was immortal in the swamp
herbage seems here crowded into smaller compass,
the concentrated greenness of the swamp. How dear
they must be to the chickadee and the rabbit! the cool,
slowly retreating rear-guard of the swamp army."

46. FRAGRANT SHIELD FERN

Aspidium fragrans (*Dryopteris fragrans*)

Northern New England to Wisconsin and northward, on rocks.
Five to sixteen inches long, with very chaffy stalks having
brown, glossy scales.

Fronds.—Lance-shaped, tapering to a point, nearly twice-pinnate,
fragrant ; *pinnæ* oblong-lanceolate, pinnatifid ; *fruit-dots* round,
large ; *indusium* large and thin.

The Fragrant Shield Fern thrives in a colder
climate than that chosen by many of its kinsmen.
Though found in the White Mountains, in the
Green Mountains (where it climbs to an elevation
of four thousand feet), in the Adirondacks, and in
other special localities of about the same latitude,
yet it is rare till we journey farther north. It loves
the crevices of shaded cliffs or mossy rocks, often
thriving best in the neighborhood of rushing brooks
and waterfalls. Frequently it seems to seek the most
inaccessible spots, as if anxious to evade discovery.
Mr. J. A. Bates, of Randolph, Vt., writes that he first
saw this little plant through a telescope from the
piazza of the Summit House on Mount Mansfield on
an apparently inaccessible ledge, the only instance in
my experience when the fern student has sought this
method of observation, suggesting " Ferns Through
a Spy-glass " as a companion volume to " Birds
Through an Opera-glass." But even the most carefully chosen spots are not safe from invasion, as Mr.
Bates tells us, for some unprincipled persons, having
felled neighboring trees and constructed a rude lad-

PLATE XXXIII

FRAGRANT SHIELD FERN
a Portion of fertile pinna

179

der, have succeeded in uprooting every plant
from the Fragrant Shield Fern Cliff on Mount
Mansfield.

The fronds of the Fragrant Shield Fern grow in a
crown and the fertile ones fruit in great abundance.

Eaton writes as follows touching the fragrance of
this fern and its use as a beverage :

" The pleasant odor of this plant remains many
years in the herbarium.   The early writers compare
the fragrance to that of raspberries, and Milde repeats
the observation.   Hooker and Greville thought it
'not unlike that of the common primrose.'   Maxi-
mowicz states that the odor is sometimes lacking.
Milde quotes Redowsky as saying that the Yakoots
of Siberia use the plant in place of tea ; and, having
tried the experiment myself, I can testify to the not
unpleasant and very fragrant astringency of the
infusion."

The following delightful description of the Fragrant Shield Fern was written by Mr. C. G. Pringle,
and is taken from Meehan's " Native Flowers and
Ferns " :

" In the several stations of *Aspidium fragrans*
among the Green Mountains which I have explored,
the plant is always seen growing from the crevices
or on the narrow shelves of dry cliffs—not often
such cliffs as are exposed to the sunlight, unless it
be on the summits of the mountains, but usually
such cliffs as are shaded by firs, and notably such
as overhang mountain-rivulets and waterfalls. When
I visit such places in summer, the niches occupied

by the plants are quite dry.   I think it would be
fatal to the plant if much spray should fall on it
during the season of its active growth.   When you
enter the shade and solitude of the haunts of this
fern, its presence is betrayed by its resinous odor;
looking up the face of the cliff, usually mottled with
lichens and moss, you see it often far above your
reach hanging against the rock, masses of dead
brown fronds, the accumulations of many years, preserved by the resinous principle which pervades
them; for the fronds, as they disport regularly
about the elongating caudex, fall right and left pre-
cisely like a woman's hair.   Above the tuft of droop-
ing dead fronds, which radiate from the centre of
the plant, grow from six to twenty green fronds,
which represent the growth of the season, those of
the preceding year dying toward autumn."

47. BRAUN'S HOLLY FERN

Aspidium aculeatum, var. Braunii (Dryopteris Braunii)

Canada to Maine, the mountains of Pennsylvania and westward, in deep rocky woods. One to more than two feet long, with chaffy stalks, having brown scales.

Fronds.—Thick, twice-pinnate; *pinnæ* lanceolate, tapering both ways; *pinnules* covered with hairs and scales, truncate, nearly rectangular at the base; *fruit-dots* roundish, small, mostly near the midveins; *indusium* orbicular, entire.

This fern is said to have been first discovered by Frederick Pursh in 1807 in Smuggler's Notch, Mount Mansfield, Vt. In the Green Mountains and in the Catskills several stations have been established. It has been found also in the Adirondacks and in Oswego County, N. Y., and it is now reported as common in the rocky woods of northern Maine, and by mountain brooks in northern New England.

Braun's Holly Fern is one of the numerous varieties of the Prickly Shield Fern or *A. aculeatum (D. aculeata)*.

Though few of our fern-students will have an opportunity to follow the Prickly Shield Fern through all the forms it assumes in different parts of the world, yet undoubtedly many of them will have the pleasure of seeing in one of its lonely and lovely haunts our own variety, Braun's Holly Fern.

PLATE XXXIV

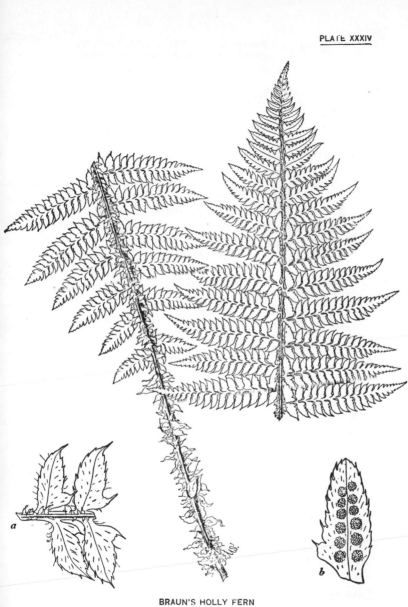

BRAUN'S HOLLY FERN

a Portion of pinna   *b* Fertile pinnule, indusia gone

48. COMMON POLYPODY. SNAKE FERN

Polypodium vulgare

Almost throughout North America, on rocks.   A few inches to
more than a foot high.

Fronds.—Oblong, smooth, somewhat
leathery, cut into narrowly oblong, usually
obtuse divisions which almost reach the
rachis ; *fruit-dots* large, round, half-way
between the midrib and margin ; *indusium*, none.

Strangely enough, the Polypody, one of our most abundant
and ubiquitous ferns, is not
rightly named, if it is noticed
at all, by nine out of ten people
who come across
it in the woods
or along the road-
side. Yet the plant
has a charm peculiarly
its own, a charm aris-
ing partly from its vig-
or, from the freshness
of its youth and
the endurance of
its old age, partly
from its odd out-
lines, and partly
from its usual en-
vironment, which

Polypody

184

entitles it to a more ready and universal recognition.

"The cheerful community of the polypody," as Thoreau calls it, thrives best on the flat surfaces of rocks. I recall the base of certain great cliffs where the rocky fragments, looking as though hurled from **above** by playful giants, are thickly covered with these plants, their rich foliage softening into beauty otherwise rugged outlines. Usually the plant is found in somewhat shaded places. Occasionally it grows on the trunks of trees and on fallen logs, as well as on rocks and cliffs.

A few weeks ago I found its fronds prettily curtaining the cleverly hidden nest of a pair of black and white creepers. It is with good reason that these birds are noted for their skill in concealing their dwelling-place. This special afternoon, when persuaded by their nervous chirps and flutterings about the rocky perch where I was sitting that the young ones were close by, I began an investigation of my precipitous and very slippery surroundings which was not rewarded for an hour or more. Not till I had climbed several feet over the side of the cliff to a narrow shelf below, broken through a thicket of blueberries, and pushed aside the tufts of Polypody which hid the entrance to the dark crevice in the rocks beyond, did I discover the little nest holding the baby creepers.

Tip of fertile frond

185

Thoreau writes of the Polypody with peculiar
sympathy:

" It is very pleasant and cheerful nowadays, when
the brown and withered leaves strew the ground
and almost every plant is fallen withered, to come
upon a patch of polypody . . . on some rocky
hill-side in the woods, where, in the midst of dry
and rustling leaves, defying frost, it stands so
freshly green and full of life. The mere greenness,
which was not remarkable in the summer, is posi-
tively interesting now. My thoughts are with the
polypody a long time after my body has passed.
. . . Why is not this form copied by our sculp-
tors instead of the foreign acanthus leaves and
bays? How fit for a tuft about the base of a col-
umn! The sight of this unwithering green leaf ex-
cites me like red at some seasons. Are not wood-
frogs the philosophers who frequent these groves?
Methinks I imbibe a cool, composed, frog-like philosophy when I behold them. The form of the polypody is strangely interesting, it is even outlandish.
Some forms, though common in our midst, are thus
perennially foreign as the growth of other latitudes.
. . . The bare outline of the polypody thrills me
strangely. It only perplexes me. Simple as it is, it
is as strange as an oriental character. It is quite
independent of my race and of the Indian, and of
all mankind. It is a fabulous, mythological form,
such as prevailed when the earth and air and
water were inhabited by those extinct fossil creat-
ures that we find. It is contemporary with them,

186

and affects us somewhat as the sight of them
might do."

49. LONG BEECH FERN

Phegopteris polypodioides (*P. Phegopteris*)

Newfoundland to Alaska, south to mountains of
Virginia, wet woods and hill-sides. Six or eight inches
to more than a foot high.

Fronds.—Triangular, usually longer than broad
(4–9 inches long, 3–6 inches broad), downy, especially
beneath, thin, once-pinnate ; *pinnæ* lance-shaped, the
lower pair noticeably standing forward and deflexed,
cut into oblong, obtuse seg-
ments ; *fruit-dots* small, round,
near the margin ; *indusium*,
none.

Of the three species
of *Phegopteris* native to
the northeastern States
P. polypodioides, com-
monly called the Long
Beech Fern, is the one
I happen to have en-
countered oftenest.

It is a less delicate
plant than either of its
sisters, the effect of the
larger and older specimens being
rather hardy, yet its downy, often
light-green, triangular frond is ex-
ceedingly pretty, with a certain oddity of aspect which it owes to the

Long Beech Fern

187

lowest pair of pinnæ, these being conspicuously deflexed and turned forward.   This peculiarity gives it a decided individuality and renders it easy of identification.

The Long Beech Fern I have found growing

a Portion of pinna   b Tip of pinna

alternately in company with the Oak Fern and the Broad Beech Fern. It loves the damp woods, clambering over the roots of trees or carpeting thickly the hollows that lie between.

50. BROAD BEECH FERN. HEXAGON BEECH FERN

Phegopteris hexagonoptera

Quebec to Florida, in dry woods and on hill-sides, with stalks eight to eighteen inches long.

Fronds.—Triangular, as broad or broader than long, seven to twelve inches broad, thin, slightly hairy, often finely glandular beneath, fragrant, once-pinnate; *pinnæ*, the large, lowest ones broadest near the middle and cut nearly to the midrib into linear-oblong, obtuse segments, the middle ones lance-shaped, tapering, the upper ones oblong, obtuse, toothed or entire; *basal segments* of the pinnæ forming a continuous, many-angled wing along the main rachis; *fruit-dots* round, small, near the margin; *indusium*, none.

In many ways this plant resembles its sister, the Long Beech Fern, but usually it is a larger plant,

188

PLATE XXXV

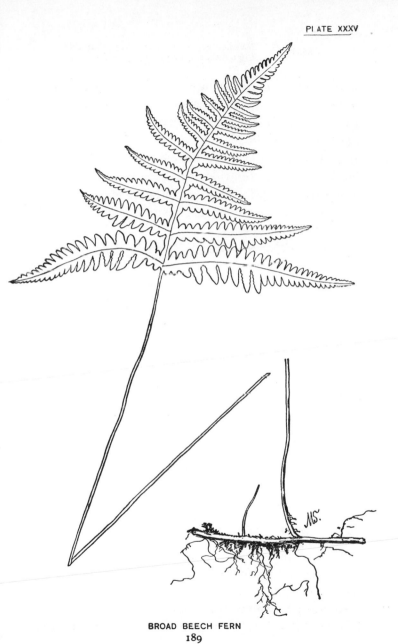

BROAD BEECH FERN
189

with more broadly triangular fronds, which wear, to
my mind, a brighter, fresher, more delicate green.
In the Long Beech Fern the two lower pairs of pinnæ differ little in length and breadth, while in the
Broad Beech Fern the lowest pair are decidedly
larger and broader than the next pair. The wing
along the rachis formed by the basal segments of the
pinnæ seems to me more conspicuous in the latter
than in the former.

The range of the Broad Beech Fern extends farther south than does that of its two kinsmen, neither
of which are found, I believe, south of Virginia. It
seeks also more open and usually drier woods. Its
leaves are fragrant.

Williamson says that its fronds are easily decolor-
ized and that they form a "good object for double-
staining, a process well known to microscopists."

51. OAK FERN

Phegopteris Dryopteris

Northeastern United States to Virginia, west to Oregon and
Alaska, usually in wet woods, with stalks six to nine inches long.

Fronds.—Usually longer than broad, four to nine inches long,
broadly triangular, the three primary divisions widely spreading,
smooth, once or twice-pinnate ; *fruit-dots* small, round, near the
margin ; *indusium*, none.

So far as I remember, my first encounter with the
Oak Fern was in a cedar swamp, famous for its
growth of showy lady's-slippers. One July day
in the hope of finding in flower some of these

PLATE XXXVI

OAK FERN

191

orchids, I visited this swamp. It lay in a semi-twilight, caused by the dense growth of cedars and hemlocks. Prostrate on the spongy sphagnum below were hosts of uprooted trees, so overrun with trailing strands of partridge-vine, twin-flower, gold-thread, and creeping snowberry, and so soft and yielding to the feet that they seemed to have become one with the earth. The stumps and far-reaching roots of the trees that had been cut or broken off above ground, instead of having been uprooted bodily, had also become gardens of many delicate woodland growths. Some of these decaying stumps and outspreading roots were thickly clothed with the clover-like leaflets of the wood-sorrel, here and there nestling among them a pink-veined blossom. On others I found side by side gleaming wild strawberries and dwarf raspberries, feathery fronds of Maidenhair, tall Osmundas, the Crested and the Spinulose Shield Ferns, the leaves of the violet, foam-flower, mitrewort, and many others of the smaller, wood-loving plants. Among these stumps were pools of water filled with the dark, polished, rounded leaves of the wild calla, and bordered by beds of moss which cushioned the equally shining but long and pointed leaves of the *Clintonia*. Near one of these pools grew a patch of delicate, low-spreading plants, evidently ferns. It needed only one searching look at the broad, triangular, light-green fronds—suggesting somewhat those of a small Brake—with roundish fruit-dots below to assure me that I had found the **Oak Fern.**

Every lover of plants or of birds or of any natural objects will appreciate the sense of something more exciting than satisfaction which I experienced as I knelt above the little plantation and gathered a few slender-stemmed fronds. One such find as this compensates for many hours of fatigue and discomfort, or intensifies the enjoyment of an already happy day. The expedition had justified itself with the first full view of the solemn, beautiful depths of the cedar forest. The discovery of the Oak Fern provided a tangible token of what we had accomplished, and when finally we found the tall, leafy plants of the showy lady's-slipper, without a single blossom left upon them, our disappointment was so mild as to be almost imperceptible.

As is often the case, having once discovered the haunt of the Oak Fern, it ceased to be a rarity. It joined the host of plants which climbed over the mossy stumps and fallen logs, and at times it fairly carpeted the ground beneath the cedars and hemlocks.

52. BULBLET BLADDER FERN

Cystopteris bulbifera

Canada to Tennessee, on wet rocks, preferring limestone. One to three feet long, with light-colored, somewhat brittle stalks.

Fronds.—Elongated, lance-shaped from a broad base, often bearing beneath large, fleshy bulbs, usually twice-pinnate; *pinnæ* lance-oblong, pointed; *pinnules* toothed or deeply lobed; *fruit-dots* roundish, *indusium* short, hood-like, attached by a broad base on the side toward the midrib, early thrown back and withering so that the mature fruit-dots appear arched.

The Bulblet Bladder Fern is never more at home than when it grows close to falling water, clinging to rocks dark and wet with spray. It seems to reflect

PLATE XXXVII

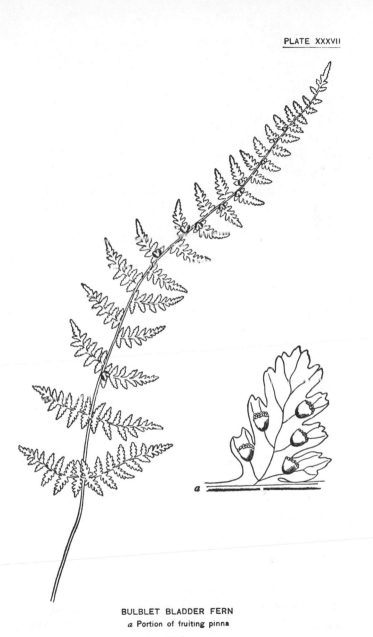

BULBLET BLADDER FERN
a Portion of fruiting pinna

195

the very spirit of the waterfall, all its life and grace, as it springs from the dripping ledges, clothing them with a diaphanous garment of delicate green which vies with their neighboring veil of white, now pouring over some rocky shelf a solid but silent mass of pale luxuriant foliage, now trailing down the cliff its long, tapering fronds, side by side with silvery strands of water, close to tufts of wind-blown, spray-tipped hare-bells.

Although the plant is never seen at its best save in some such neighborhood as this, its slender, feathery fronds are always possessed of singular grace and charm, whether undulating along the dried rocky bed of a mountain brook or bending till their slender tips nearly touch the rushing stream or growing quite away from the rocks which are their natural and usual companions among the moss-grown trunks and fallen trees of the wet woods.

I know no other fern, save the climbing fern, which is so vine-like and clinging. In reality its stalk and midrib are somewhat brittle, yet this brittleness does not prevent its adapting itself with supple and exquisite curves to whatever support it has chosen.

In its manner of growth, as well as in its slender, tapering outline, the Bulblet Bladder Fern is so individual that there can be no difficulty in identifying the full-sized fertile fronds, even in the absence of the little bulbs which grow on the under side of the frond, usually at the base of the pinnæ. The sterile

PLATE XXXVIII

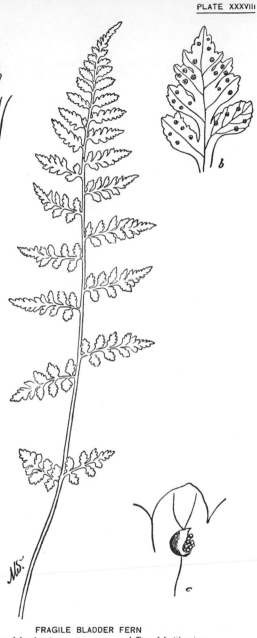

FRAGILE BLADDER FERN

a Portion of fertile pinna   *b* Tip of fertile pinna

c Magnified fruit-dot showing indusium

fronds are shorter and broader in proportion, and
not so easily identified.

53. FRAGILE BLADDER FERN. COMMON BLADDER FERN

Cystopteris fragilis

A rock and wood fern, found from Newfoundland to Georgia.
Six to eighteen inches long, with slender and brittle stalks, green
except at the base.

Fronds.—Oblong-lanceolate, thin, twice to thrice-pinnate or pinnatifid ; *pinnæ* lance-ovate, irregularly cut into toothed segments
which at their base run along the midrib by a narrow margin ; *fruit-
dots* roundish, often abundant; *indusium* early withering and
exposing the sporangia, which finally appear naked.

This plant may be ranked among the earliest ferns
of the year. In May or June, if we climb down to
the brook where the columbine flings out her brilliant, nodding blossoms, we find the delicate little
fronds, just uncurled, clinging to the steep, moist
rocks, or perhaps beyond, in the deeper woods, they
nestle among the spreading roots of some great forest tree. Their "fragile greenness" is very winning.
As the plant matures, attaining at times a height of
nearly two feet, it loses something of this first delicate charm. By the end of July its fruit has ripened,
its spores are discharged, and the plant disappears.
Frequently, if not always, a new crop springs up in
August. We are enchanted to discover tender
young fronds making patches of fresh green in every crevice of the rocks among which the stream
forces its precipitous way. Once more the woods
are flavored with the essence of spring. In our

PLATE XXXiX

RUSTY WOODSIA

delight in this new promise we forget for a moment to mourn the vanishing summer.

The outline of the Common Bladder Fern suggests that of the Obtuse Woodsia. The two plants might be difficult to distinguish were it not for the difference in their indusia. At maturity the indusium of the Common Bladder Fern usually disappears, leaving the fruit-dot naked, while that of the Obtuse Woodsia is fastened underneath the fruit-dot and splits apart into jagged, spreading lobes.

The sterile fronds of the Slender Cliff Brake also have been thought to resemble this fern, in whose company it often grows.

Williamson says that the Common Bladder Fern is easily cultivated either in mounds or on rock-work.

54. RUSTY WOODSIA

Woodsia Ilvensis

From Labrador and Greenland south to North Carolina and Kentucky, usually on exposed rocks in somewhat mountainous regions. A few inches to nearly one foot high.

Fronds.—Oblong-lance-shaped, rather smooth above, the stalk and under surface of the frond thickly clothed with rusty chaff, once-pinnate ; *pinnæ* oblong, obtuse, sessile, cut into oblong segments ; *fruit-dots* round, near the margin, often confluent at maturity ; *indusium* detached by its base under the sporangia, dividing into slender hairs which curl above them.

Last Decoration Day, while clambering over some rocky cliffs in the Berkshire Hills, I found the Rusty Woodsia growing in masses so luxuriant to the eye and so velvety to the touch that it hardly

PLATE XL

BLUNT-LOBED WOODSIA

a Portion of pinna   *b* Fruit-dot magnified, showing indusium

201

suggested the bristly looking plant which one finds later in the summer.

This fern reverses the usual order of things, being gray-haired in youth and brown-haired in old age, with the result that in May its effect is a soft, silvery green. But even in August, if you chance upon a vigorous tuft springing from some rocky crevice, despite its lack of delicacy and its bristle of red-brown hairs or chaff, the plant is an attractive one.

Environment has much to do with the charm of ferns. The first plant of this species I ever identified grew on a rocky shelf within a few feet of a stream which flowed swift and cold from the near mountains. Close by, from the forked branches of a crimson-fruited mountain maple, hung the dainty, deserted nest of a vireo. Always the Rusty Woodsia seems to bring me a message from that abode of solitude and silence.

55. BLUNT-LOBED WOODSIA

Woodsia obtusa

Canada to Georgia and Alabama and westward, on rocks. Eight to twenty inches high, with stalks not jointed, chaffy when young.

Fronds.—Broadly lanceolate, nearly twice-pinnate ; *pinnæ* rather remote, triangular-ovate or oblong, pinnately parted into obtuse, oblong, toothed segments ; *veins* forked ; *fruit-dots* on or near the minutely toothed lobes ; *indusium* conspicuous, splitting into several jagged lobes.

The Blunt-lobed Woodsia is not rare on rocks and stony hillsides in Maine and Northern New York.

It is found frequently in the valley of the **Hudson**.
Though not related to the Common Bladder Fern
(*C. fragilis*), it has somewhat the same general appearance. Its fronds, however, are usually both
broader and longer, and its stalk and pinnæ are
slightly downy. Its range does not vary greatly
from that of the Common Bladder Fern, but
usually it grows in more exposed spots and sometimes basks in strong sunshine.

Meehan says the Blunt-lobed Woodsia is found
along the Wissahickon Creek, Penna., on dry walls
in shady places. " One of its happiest phases,"
he continues, " is toward the fall of the year, when
the short, barren fronds which form the outer circle
bend downward, forming a sort of rosette, in the
centre of which the fertile fronds somewhat erectly
stand."

The sterile fronds remain fairly green till spring.

56. NORTHERN WOODSIA. ALPINE WOODSIA

Woodsia hyperborea (*W. alpina*)

Northern New York and Vermont, and northward from Labrador to Alaska, on rocks. Two to six inches long, with stalks
jointed near the base.

Fronds.—Narrowly oblong-lanceolate, nearly smooth, pinnate ;
pinnæ triangular-ovate, obtuse, lobed ; *lobes* few ; *fruit-dots* somewhat scattered ; *indusium* as in *W. Ilvensis.*

This rare little fern has been found by Dr. Peck
in the Adirondacks and by Horace Mann, jr., and
Mr. Pringle in Vermont. In his delightful " Rem-

iniscences of Botanical Rambles in Vermont,"
published in the Torrey *Bulletin*, July, 1897, Mr.
Pringle describes his first discovery of this species :

" I was on the mountain [Willoughby] on the 4th
of August and examined the entire length of the
cliffs, climbing upon all their accessible shelves.
Among the specimens of *Woodsia glabella* brought
away were a few which I judged to belong to a
different species. Mr. Frost, to whom they were
first submitted, pronounced them *Woodsia glabella*.
Not satisfied with his report, I showed them to Dr.
Gray. By him I was advised to send them to Professor Eaton, because, as he said, *Woodsia* is a criti-
cal genus. Professor Eaton assured me that I had
Woodsia hyperborea, . . . another addition to the
flora of the United States."

Later in the year Mr. Pringle made a visit to
Smugglers' Notch on Mount Mansfield, when he was
"prepared to camp in the old Notch House among
hedgehogs, and botanize the region day by day."
This visit was rich in its results. The most nota-
ble finds were *Aspidium fragrans*, *Asplenium viride*,
Woodsia glabella, and *Woodsia hyperborea*.

PLATE XLi

NORTHERN WOODSIA

57. SMOOTH WOODSIA

Woodsia glabella

Northern New York and Vermont, and northward from Labrador to Alaska, on moist rocks. Two to five inches long, with stalks jointed at base.

Fronds.—Very delicate, linear or narrowly lanceolate, smooth on both sides, pinnate ; *pinnæ* roundish ovate, obtuse, lobed, lobes few ; *fruit-dots* scattered ; *indusium* minute.

The Smooth Woodsia closely resembles the Northern Woodsia, and one may expect to find it in much the same parts of the country. In texture it is still more delicate ; its fronds are almost perfectly smooth, its outline is narrower, and its pinnæ are but slightly lobed.

Mr. Pringle tells us that a letter from Mr. George Davenport, asking him to look for *Woodsia glabella*, awakened his first interest in ferns. His own account of these early fern hunts is inspiring in its enthusiasm :

" In 1873 George Davenport was beginning his study of ferns. A letter from him, asking me to look for *Woodsia glabella* . . . started me on a fern hunt. The species had been found on Willoughby Mountain, Vt., and at Little Falls, N. Y.; might it not be growing in many places in Vermont? When I set out I knew, as I must suppose, not a single fern, and it was near the close of the summer. You can imagine what delights awaited me in the autumn woodlands. I made the acquaintance of not a few ferns, though it was too late to prepare good specimens of them. In this first blind endeavor I got, of

PLATE XLII

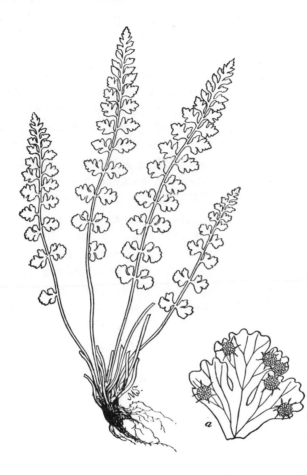

SMOOTH WOODSIA
a Fertile pinna
207

course, no clew to *Woodsia glabella*. The next summer the hunt was renewed and persistently followed
up. I found pleasure in securing one by one nearly
all our Vermont ferns. At the time I thought it
worthy of remembrance that a single field of diversi-
fied pasture and woodland on an adjoining farm
yielded me thirty species. Although the two common species of *Woodsia* were near at hand, *Woodsia
glabella* was still eluding my search. I sent a friend
to the summit of Jay Peak in a fruitless quest for it.
Finally, on September 1st, I joined Mr. Congdon at
its old station on Willoughby Mountain, and made
myself familiar with its exquisite form.

"During the first two years of my collecting in
earnest, 1874 and 1875, several visits were made to
Camel's Hump, the peak most accessible to me. In
this way some time was lost, because its subalpine
area is limited, and consequently the number of rare
plants to be found there is small. Yet, with such
dogged persistence as sometimes prevents my making good progress, my last visit to that point was
not made till the 20th of June, 1876. On that day I
clambered, I believe, over every shelf of its great
southern precipice and peered into every fissure
among the rocks. At last, as I was climbing up the
apex over the southeastern buttress, my perilous toil
was rewarded by the discovery not only of *Woodsia
glabella*, but of *Aspidium fragrans*. . . . There
were only a few depauperate specimens of each
which had not yet succumbed to the adverse conditions of their dry and exposed situation."

In the following passage Mr. Pringle describes his
pleasure, some years later, in the companionships
fostered by a common interest in his pet hobby:

". . . my delight in this preserve of boreal
plants was shared with not a few genial botanists.
Charles Faxon came before any of us suspected that
he possessed undeveloped talent for a botanical ar-
tist of highest excellence. Edwin Faxon followed
his young brother, and with me made the tedious ascent to Stirling Pond, a day of toil well rewarded.
Thomas Morong came, before the hardships of his
Paraguayan journey had broken him down. . . .
Our honored President came. . . . In those days,
as now, . . . he was often my companion to add
delight to my occupation and to reinforce my enthusiasm. . . . The gentle Davenport came at
last to behold for the first time in their native haunts
many of the objects of his first love and study. When
I had found for him yet once more in a fifth Vermont
station (this was under Checkerberry Ledge, near
Bakersfield) the fern he at first desired, and, together
with that, had discovered within our limits three or
four others quite as rare and scarcely expected, I
might feel that I had complied with the request of his
letter. But that letter initiated a warm friendship
between us and association in work upon American
ferns, which has continued to the present time.
During these twenty-three years of botanical travel
on my part my hands have gathered all but thirty-
six of the one hundred and sixty-five species of North
American ferns, and from the more remote corners

of our continent I have sent home to my friend for
description and publication sixteen new ones. Yet
I trust that the fern hunt upon which he started me
in 1873 is still far from its close."

The above quotations illustrate fairly the enthusiasm aroused by a pursuit which is full of peculiar
fascination. Almost anyone who has made a study
of our native ferns will recall hours filled with delight through their agency, companions made more
companionable by means of a common interest in
their names, haunts, and habits.

INDEX TO LATIN NAMES

INDEX TO ENGLISH NAMES

INDEX TO TECHNICAL TERMS

A CATALOGUE OF SELECTED DOVER BOOKS
IN ALL FIELDS OF INTEREST

A CATALOGUE OF SELECTED DOVER BOOKS
IN ALL FIELDS OF INTEREST

WHAT IS SCIENCE?, *N. Campbell*
The role of experiment and measurement, the function of mathematics, the nature of scientific laws, the difference between laws and theories, the limitations of science, and many similarly provocative topics are treated clearly and without technicalities by an eminent scientist. "Still an excellent introduction to scientific philosophy," H. Margenau in *Physics Today*. "A first-rate primer . . . deserves a wide audience," *Scientific American*. 192pp. 5⅜ x 8.
60043-2 Paperbound $1.25

THE NATURE OF LIGHT AND COLOUR IN THE OPEN AIR, *M. Minnaert*
Why are shadows sometimes blue, sometimes green, or other colors depending on the light and surroundings? What causes mirages? Why do multiple suns and moons appear in the sky? Professor Minnaert explains these unusual phenomena and hundreds of others in simple, easy-to-understand terms based on optical laws and the properties of light and color. No mathematics is required but artists, scientists, students, and everyone fascinated by these "tricks" of nature will find thousands of useful and amazing pieces of information. Hundreds of observational experiments are suggested which require no special equipment. 200 illustrations; 42 photos. xvi + 362pp. 5⅜ x 8.
20196-1 Paperbound $2.00

THE STRANGE STORY OF THE QUANTUM, AN ACCOUNT FOR THE GENERAL READER OF THE GROWTH OF IDEAS UNDERLYING OUR PRESENT ATOMIC KNOWLEDGE, *B. Hoffmann*
Presents lucidly and expertly, with barest amount of mathematics, the problems and theories which led to modern quantum physics. Dr. Hoffmann begins with the closing years of the 19th century, when certain trifling discrepancies were noticed, and with illuminating analogies and examples takes you through the brilliant concepts of Planck, Einstein, Pauli, Broglie, Bohr, Schroedinger, Heisenberg, Dirac, Sommerfeld, Feynman, etc. This edition includes a new, long postscript carrying the story through 1958. "Of the books attempting an account of the history and contents of our modern atomic physics which have come to my attention, this is the best," H. Margenau, Yale University, in *American Journal of Physics*. 32 tables and line illustrations. Index. 275pp. 5⅜ x 8.
20518-5 Paperbound $2.00

GREAT IDEAS OF MODERN MATHEMATICS: THEIR NATURE AND USE, *Jagjit Singh*
Reader with only high school math will understand main mathematical ideas of modern physics, astronomy, genetics, psychology, evolution, etc. better than many who use them as tools, but comprehend little of their basic structure. Author uses his wide knowledge of non-mathematical fields in brilliant exposition of differential equations, matrices, group theory, logic, statistics, problems of mathematical foundations, imaginary numbers, vectors, etc. Original publication. 2 appendixes. 2 indexes. 65 ills. 322pp. 5⅜ x 8.
20587-8 Paperbound $2.25

THE METHODS OF ETHICS, *Henry Sidgwick*
Propounding no organized system of its own, study subjects every major methodological approach to ethics to rigorous, objective analysis. Study discusses and relates ethical thought of Plato, Aristotle, Bentham, Clarke, Butler, Hobbes, Hume, Mill, Spencer, Kant, and dozens of others. Sidgwick retains conclusions from each system which follow from ethical premises, rejecting the faulty. Considered by many in the field to be among the most important treatises on ethical philosophy. Appendix. Index. xlvii + 528pp. 5⅜ x 8½.
21608-X Paperbound $2.50

TEUTONIC MYTHOLOGY, *Jakob Grimm*
A milestone in Western culture; the work which established on a modern basis the study of history of religions and comparative religions. 4-volume work assembles and interprets everything available on religious and folkloristic beliefs of Germanic people (including Scandinavians, Anglo-Saxons, etc.). Assembling material from such sources as Tacitus, surviving Old Norse and Icelandic texts, archeological remains, folktales, surviving superstitions, comparative traditions, linguistic analysis, etc. Grimm explores pagan deities, heroes, folklore of nature, religious practices, and every other area of pagan German belief. To this day, the unrivaled, definitive, exhaustive study. Translated by J. S. Stallybrass from 4th (1883) German edition. Indexes. Total of lxxvii + 1887pp. 5⅜ x 8½.
21602-0, 21603-9, 21604-7, 21605-5 Four volume set, paperbound $11.00

THE I CHING, *translated by James Legge*
Called "The Book of Changes" in English, this is one of the Five Classics edited by Confucius, basic and central to Chinese thought. Explains perhaps the most complex system of divination known, founded on the theory that all things happening at any one time have characteristic features which can be isolated and related. Significant in Oriental studies, in history of religions and philosophy, and also to Jungian psychoanalysis and other areas of modern European thought. Index. Appendixes. 6 plates. xxi + 448pp. 5⅜ x 8½.
21062-6 Paperbound $2.75

HISTORY OF ANCIENT PHILOSOPHY, *W. Windelband*
One of the clearest, most accurate comprehensive surveys of Greek and Roman philosophy. Discusses ancient philosophy in general, intellectual life in Greece in the 7th and 6th centuries B.C., Thales, Anaximander, Anaximenes, Heraclitus, the Eleatics, Empedocles, Anaxagoras, Leucippus, the Pythagoreans, the Sophists, Socrates, Democritus (20 pages), Plato (50 pages), Aristotle (70 pages), the Peripatetics, Stoics, Epicureans, Sceptics, Neo-platonists, Christian Apologists, etc. 2nd German edition translated by H. E. Cushman. xv + 393pp. 5⅜ x 8.
20357-3 Paperbound $2.25

THE PALACE OF PLEASURE, *William Painter*
Elizabethan versions of Italian and French novels from *The Decameron*, Cinthio, Straparola, Queen Margaret of Navarre, and other continental sources — the very work that provided Shakespeare and dozens of his contemporaries with many of their plots and sub-plots and, therefore, justly considered one of the most influential books in all English literature. It is also a book that any reader will still enjoy. Total of cviii + 1,224pp.
21691-8, 21692-6, 21693-4 Three volume set, paperbound $6.75

THE PRINCIPLES OF PSYCHOLOGY,
William James
The full long-course, unabridged, of one of the great classics of Western literature and science. Wonderfully lucid descriptions of human mental activity, the stream of thought, consciousness, time perception, memory, imagination, emotions, reason, abnormal phenomena, and similar topics. Original contributions are integrated with the work of such men as Berkeley, Binet, Mills, Darwin, Hume, Kant, Royce, Schopenhauer, Spinoza, Locke, Descartes, Galton, Wundt, Lotze, Herbart, Fechner, and scores of others. All contrasting interpretations of mental phenomena are examined in detail—introspective analysis, philosophical interpretation, and experimental research. "A classic," *Journal of Consulting Psychology.* "The main lines are as valid as ever," *Psychoanalytical Quarterly.* "Standard reading . . . a classic of interpretation," *Psychiatric Quarterly.* 94 illustrations. 1408pp. 5⅜ x 8.
20381-6, 20382-4 Two volume set, paperbound $6.00

VISUAL ILLUSIONS: THEIR CAUSES, CHARACTERISTICS AND APPLICATIONS,
M. Luckiesh
"Seeing is deceiving," asserts the author of this introduction to virtually every type of optical illusion known. The text both describes and explains the principles involved in color illusions, figure-ground, distance illusions, etc. 100 photographs, drawings and diagrams prove how easy it is to fool the sense: circles that aren't round, parallel lines that seem to bend, stationary figures that seem to move as you stare at them — illustration after illustration strains our credulity at what we see. Fascinating book from many points of view, from applications for artists, in camouflage, etc. to the psychology of vision. New introduction by William Ittleson, Dept. of Psychology, Queens College. Index. Bibliography. xxi + 252pp. 5⅜ x 8½.
21530-X Paperbound $1.50

FADS AND FALLACIES IN THE NAME OF SCIENCE,
Martin Gardner
This is the standard account of various cults, quack systems, and delusions which have masqueraded as science: hollow earth fanatics. Reich and orgone sex energy, dianetics, Atlantis, multiple moons, Forteanism, flying saucers, medical fallacies like iridiagnosis, zone therapy, etc. A new chapter has been added on Bridey Murphy, psionics, and other recent manifestations in this field. This is a fair, reasoned appraisal of eccentric theory which provides excellent inoculation against cleverly masked nonsense. "Should be read by everyone, scientist and non-scientist alike," R. T. Birge, Prof. Emeritus of Physics, Univ. of California; Former President, American Physical Society. Index. x + 365pp. 5⅜ x 8.
20394-8 Paperbound $2.00

ILLUSIONS AND DELUSIONS OF THE SUPERNATURAL AND THE OCCULT,
D. H. Rawcliffe
Holds up to rational examination hundreds of persistent delusions including crystal gazing, automatic writing, table turning, mediumistic trances, mental healing, stigmata, lycanthropy, live burial, the Indian Rope Trick, spiritualism, dowsing, telepathy, clairvoyance, ghosts, ESP, etc. The author explains and exposes the mental and physical deceptions involved, making this not only an exposé of supernatural phenomena, but a valuable exposition of characteristic types of abnormal psychology. Originally titled "The Psychology of the Occult." 14 illustrations. Index. 551pp. 5⅜ x 8. 20503-7 Paperbound $3.50

CELESTIAL OBJECTS FOR COMMON TELESCOPES,
Rev. T. W. Webb
Classic handbook for the use and pleasure of the amateur astronomer. Of
inestimable aid in locating and identifying thousands of celestial objects. Vol I,
The Solar System: discussions of the principle and operation of the telescope,
procedures of observations and telescope-photography, spectroscopy, etc., precise
location information of sun, moon, planets, meteors. Vol. II, The Stars:
alphabetical listing of constellations, information on double stars, clusters, stars
with unusual spectra, variables, and nebulae, etc. Nearly 4,000 objects noted.
Edited and extensively revised by Margaret W. Mayall, director of the American
Assn. of Variable Star Observers. New Index by Mrs. Mayall giving the location
of all objects mentioned in the text for Epoch 2000. New Precession Table
added. New appendices on the planetary satellites, constellation names and
abbreviations, and solar system data. Total of 46 illustrations. Total of xxxix
+ 606pp. 5⅜ x 8.   20917-2, 20918-0 Two volume set, paperbound $5.00

PLANETARY THEORY,
E. W. Brown and C. A. Shook
Provides a clear presentation of basic methods for calculating planetary orbits
for today's astronomer. Begins with a careful exposition of specialized mathematical topics essential for handling perturbation theory and then goes on to
indicate how most of the previous methods reduce ultimately to two general
calculation methods: obtaining expressions either for the coordinates of planetary positions or for the elements which determine the perturbed paths. An
example of each is given and worked in detail. Corrected edition. Preface.
Appendix. Index. xii + 302pp. 5⅜ x 8½.   61133-7 Paperbound $2.25

STAR NAMES AND THEIR MEANINGS,
Richard Hinckley Allen
An unusual book documenting the various attributions of names to the
individual stars over the centuries. Here is a treasure-house of information on
a topic not normally delved into even by professional astronomers; provides a
fascinating background to the stars in folk-lore, literary references, ancient
writings, star catalogs and maps over the centuries. Constellation-by-constella-
tion analysis covers hundreds of stars and other asterisms, including the
Pleiades, Hyades, Andromedan Nebula, etc. Introduction. Indices. List of
authors and authorities. xx + 563pp. 5⅜ x 8½.   21079-0 Paperbound $3.00

A SHORT HISTORY OF ASTRONOMY, *A. Berry*
Popular standard work for over 50 years, this thorough and accurate volume
covers the science from primitive times to the end of the 19th century. After
the Greeks and the Middle Ages, individual chapters analyze Copernicus, Brahe,
Galileo, Kepler, and Newton, and the mixed reception of their discoveries.
Post-Newtonian achievements are then discussed in unusual detail: Halley,
Bradley, Lagrange, Laplace, Herschel, Bessel, etc. 2 Indexes. 104 illustrations,
9 portraits. xxxi + 440pp. 5⅜ x 8.   20210-0 Paperbound $2.75

SOME THEORY OF SAMPLING, *W. E. Deming*
The purpose of this book is to make sampling techniques understandable to
and useable by social scientists, industrial managers, and natural scientists
who are finding statistics increasingly part of their work. Over 200 exercises,
plus dozens of actual applications. 61 tables. 90 figs. xix + 602pp. 5⅜ x 8½.
          61755-6 Paperbound $3.50

FAIRY TALE COLLECTIONS, *edited by Andrew Lang*
Andrew Lang's fairy tale collections make up the richest shelf-full of traditional children's stories anywhere available. Lang supervised the translation of stories from all over the world—familiar European tales collected by Grimm, animal stories from Negro Africa, myths of primitive Australia, stories from Russia, Hungary, Iceland, Japan, and many other countries. Lang's selection of translations are unusually high; many authorities consider that the most familiar tales find their best versions in these volumes. All collections are richly decorated and illustrated by H. J. Ford and other artists.

THE BLUE FAIRY BOOK. 37 stories. 138 illustrations. ix + 390pp. 5⅜ x 8½.
21437-0 Paperbound $1.95

THE GREEN FAIRY BOOK. 42 stories. 100 illustrations. xiii + 366pp. 5⅜ x 8½.
21439-7 Paperbound $1.75

THE BROWN FAIRY BOOK. 32 stories. 50 illustrations, 8 in color. xii + 350pp. 5⅜ x 8½.
21438-9 Paperbound $1.95

THE BEST TALES OF HOFFMANN, *edited by E. F. Bleiler*
10 stories by E. T. A. Hoffmann, one of the greatest of all writers of fantasy. The tales include "The Golden Flower Pot," "Automata," "A New Year's Eve Adventure," "Nutcracker and the King of Mice," "Sand-Man," and others. Vigorous characterizations of highly eccentric personalities, remarkably imaginative situations, and intensely fast pacing has made these tales popular all over the world for 150 years. Editor's introduction. 7 drawings by Hoffmann. xxxiii + 419pp. 5⅜ x 8½.
21793-0 Paperbound $2.25

GHOST AND HORROR STORIES OF AMBROSE BIERCE,
edited by E. F. Bleiler
Morbid, eerie, horrifying tales of possessed poets, shabby aristocrats, revived corpses, and haunted malefactors. Widely acknowledged as the best of their kind between Poe and the moderns, reflecting their author's inner torment and bitter view of life. Includes "Damned Thing," "The Middle Toe of the Right Foot," "The Eyes of the Panther," "Visions of the Night," "Moxon's Master," and over a dozen others. Editor's introduction. xxii + 199pp. 5⅜ x 8½.
20767-6 Paperbound $1.50

THREE GOTHIC NOVELS, *edited by E. F. Bleiler*
Originators of the still popular Gothic novel form, influential in ushering in early 19th-century Romanticism. Horace Walpole's *Castle of Otranto*, William Beckford's *Vathek*, John Polidori's *The Vampyre*, and a *Fragment* by Lord Byron are enjoyable as exciting reading or as documents in the history of English literature. Editor's introduction. xi + 291pp. 5⅜ x 8½.
21232-7 Paperbound $2.00

BEST GHOST STORIES OF LEFANU, *edited by E. F. Bleiler*
Though admired by such critics as V. S. Pritchett, Charles Dickens and Henry James, ghost stories by the Irish novelist Joseph Sheridan LeFanu have never become as widely known as his detective fiction. About half of the 16 stories in this collection have never before been available in America. Collection includes "Carmilla" (perhaps the best vampire story ever written), "The Haunted Baronet," "The Fortunes of Sir Robert Ardagh," and the classic "Green Tea." Editor's introduction. 7 contemporary illustrations. Portrait of LeFanu. xii + 467pp. 5⅜ x 8.
20415-4 Paperbound $2.50

THREE SCIENCE FICTION NOVELS,
John Taine
Acknowledged by many as the best SF writer of the 1920's, Taine (under the name Eric Temple Bell) was also a Professor of Mathematics of considerable renown. Reprinted here are *The Time Stream*, generally considered Taine's best, *The Greatest Game*, a biological-fiction novel, and *The Purple Sapphire*, involving a supercivilization of the past. Taine's stories tie fantastic narratives to frameworks of original and logical scientific concepts. Speculation is often profound on such questions as the nature of time, concept of entropy, cyclical universes, etc. 4 contemporary illustrations. v + 532pp. 5⅜ x 8⅜.
21180-0 Paperbound $2.50

SEVEN SCIENCE FICTION NOVELS,
H. G. Wells
Full unabridged texts of 7 science-fiction novels of the master. Ranging from biology, physics, chemistry, astronomy, to sociology and other studies, Mr. Wells extrapolates whole worlds of strange and intriguing character. "One will have to go far to match this for entertainment, excitement, and sheer pleasure . . ."*New York Times.* Contents: The Time Machine, The Island of Dr. Moreau, The First Men in the Moon, The Invisible Man, The War of the Worlds, The Food of the Gods, In The Days of the Comet. 1015pp. 5⅜ x 8.
20264-X Clothbound $5.00

28 SCIENCE FICTION STORIES OF H. G. WELLS.
Two full, unabridged novels, *Men Like Gods* and *Star Begotten*, plus 26 short stories by the master science-fiction writer of all time! Stories of space, time, invention, exploration, futuristic adventure. Partial contents: *The Country of the Blind, In the Abyss, The Crystal Egg, The Man Who Could Work Miracles, A Story of Days to Come, The Empire of the Ants, The Magic Shop, The Valley of the Spiders, A Story of the Stone Age, Under the Knife, Sea Raiders,* etc. An indispensable collection for the library of anyone interested in science fiction adventure. 928pp. 5⅜ x 8.
20265-8 Clothbound $5.00

THREE MARTIAN NOVELS,
Edgar Rice Burroughs
Complete, unabridged reprinting, in one volume, of Thuvia, Maid of Mars; Chessmen of Mars; The Master Mind of Mars. Hours of science-fiction adventure by a modern master storyteller. Reset in large clear type for easy reading. 16 illustrations by J. Allen St. John. vi + 490pp. 5⅜ x 8½.
20039-6 Paperbound $2.50

AN INTELLECTUAL AND CULTURAL HISTORY OF THE WESTERN WORLD,
Harry Elmer Barnes
Monumental 3-volume survey of intellectual development of Europe from primitive cultures to the present day. Every significant product of human intellect traced through history: art, literature, mathematics, physical sciences, medicine, music, technology, social sciences, religions, jurisprudence, education, etc. Presentation is lucid and specific, analyzing in detail specific discoveries, theories, literary works, and so on. Revised (1965) by recognized scholars in specialized fields under the direction of Prof. Barnes. Revised bibliography. Indexes. 24 illustrations. Total of xxix + 1318pp.
21275-0, 21276-9, 21277-7 Three volume set, paperbound $8.25

MATHEMATICAL PHYSICS, *D. H. Menzel*
Thorough one-volume treatment of the mathematical techniques vital for classical mechanics, electromagnetic theory, quantum theory, and relativity. Written by the Harvard Professor of Astrophysics for junior, senior, and graduate courses, it gives clear explanations of all those aspects of function theory, vectors, matrices, dyadics, tensors, partial differential equations, etc., necessary for the understanding of the various physical theories. Electron theory, relativity, and other topics seldom presented appear here in considerable detail. Scores of definition, conversion factors, dimensional constants, etc. "More detailed than normal for an advanced text . . . excellent set of sections on Dyadics, Matrices, and Tensors," *Journal of the Franklin Institute.* Index. 193 problems, with answers. x + 412pp. 5⅜ x 8.   60056-4 Paperbound $2.50

THE THEORY OF SOUND, *Lord Rayleigh*
Most vibrating systems likely to be encountered in practice can be tackled successfully by the methods set forth by the great Nobel laureate, Lord Rayleigh. Complete coverage of experimental, mathematical aspects of sound theory. Partial contents: Harmonic motions, vibrating systems in general, lateral vibrations of bars, curved plates or shells, applications of Laplace's functions to acoustical problems, fluid friction, plane vortex-sheet, vibrations of solid bodies, etc. This is the first inexpensive edition of this great reference and study work. Bibliography, Historical introduction by R. B. Lindsay. Total of 1040pp. 97 figures. 5⅜ x 8.   60292-3, 60293-1 Two volume set, paperbound $6.00

HYDRODYNAMICS, *Horace Lamb*
Internationally famous complete coverage of standard reference work on dynamics of liquids & gases. Fundamental theorems, equations, methods, solutions, background, for classical hydrodynamics. Chapters include Equations of Motion, Integration of Equations in Special Gases, Irrotational Motion, Motion of Liquid in 2 Dimensions, Motion of Solids through Liquid-Dynamical Theory, Vortex Motion, Tidal Waves, Surface Waves, Waves of Expansion, Viscosity, Rotating Masses of Liquids. Excellently planned, arranged; clear, lucid presentation. 6th enlarged, revised edition. Index. Over 900 footnotes, mostly bibliographical. 119 figures. xv + 738pp. 6⅛ x 9¼.   60256-7 Paperbound $4.00

DYNAMICAL THEORY OF GASES, *James Jeans*
Divided into mathematical and physical chapters for the convenience of those not expert in mathematics, this volume discusses the mathematical theory of gas in a steady state, thermodynamics, Boltzmann and Maxwell, kinetic theory, quantum theory, exponentials, etc. 4th enlarged edition, with new material on quantum theory, quantum dynamics, etc. Indexes. 28 figures. 444pp. 6⅛ x 9¼.
60136-6 Paperbound $2.75

THERMODYNAMICS, *Enrico Fermi*
Unabridged reproduction of 1937 edition. Elementary in treatment; remarkable for clarity, organization. Requires no knowledge of advanced math beyond calculus, only familiarity with fundamentals of thermometry, calorimetry. Partial Contents: Thermodynamic systems; First & Second laws of thermodynamics; Entropy; Thermodynamic potentials: phase rule, reversible electric cell; Gaseous reactions: van't Hoff reaction box, principle of LeChatelier; Thermodynamics of dilute solutions: osmotic & vapor pressures, boiling & freezing points; Entropy constant. Index. 25 problems. 24 illustrations. x + 160pp. 5⅜ x 8.   60361-X Paperbound $2.00

EASY-TO-DO ENTERTAINMENTS AND DIVERSIONS WITH COINS, CARDS, STRING, PAPER AND MATCHES, *R. M. Abraham*

Over 300 tricks, games and puzzles will provide young readers with absorbing fun. Sections on card games; paper-folding; tricks with coins, matches and pieces of string; games for the agile; toy-making from common household objects; mathematical recreations; and 50 miscellaneous pastimes. Anyone in charge of groups of youngsters, including hard-pressed parents, and in need of suggestions on how to keep children sensibly amused and quietly content will find this book indispensable. Clear, simple text, copious number of delightful line drawings and illustrative diagrams. Originally titled "Winter Nights' Entertainments." Introduction by Lord Baden Powell. 329 illustrations. v + 186pp. 5⅜ x 8½. 20921-0 Paperbound $1.00

AN INTRODUCTION TO CHESS MOVES AND TACTICS SIMPLY EXPLAINED, *Leonard Barden*

Beginner's introduction to the royal game. Names, possible moves of the pieces, definitions of essential terms, how games are won, etc. explained in 30-odd pages. With this background you'll be able to sit right down and play. Balance of book teaches strategy — openings, middle game, typical endgame play, and suggestions for improving your game. A sample game is fully analyzed. True middle-level introduction, teaching you all the essentials without oversimplifying or losing you in a maze of detail. 58 figures. 102pp. 5⅜ x 8½. 21210-6 Paperbound $1.25

LASKER'S MANUAL OF CHESS, *Dr. Emanuel Lasker*

Probably the greatest chess player of modern times, Dr. Emanuel Lasker held the world championship 28 years, independent of passing schools or fashions. This unmatched study of the game, chiefly for intermediate to skilled players, analyzes basic methods, combinations, position play, the aesthetics of chess, dozens of different openings, etc., with constant reference to great modern games. Contains a brilliant exposition of Steinitz's important theories. Introduction by Fred Reinfeld. Tables of Lasker's tournament record. 3 indices. 308 diagrams. 1 photograph. xxx + 349pp. 5⅜ x 8. 20640-8 Paperbound $2.50

COMBINATIONS: THE HEART OF CHESS, *Irving Chernev*

Step-by-step from simple combinations to complex, this book, by a well-known chess writer, shows you the intricacies of pins, counter-pins, knight forks, and smothered mates. Other chapters show alternate lines of play to those taken in actual championship games; boomerang combinations; classic examples of brilliant combination play by Nimzovich, Rubinstein, Tarrasch, Botvinnik, Alekhine and Capablanca. Index. 356 diagrams. ix + 245pp. 5⅜ x 8½. 21744-2 Paperbound $2.00

HOW TO SOLVE CHESS PROBLEMS, *K. S. Howard*

Full of practical suggestions for the fan or the beginner — who knows only the moves of the chessmen. Contains preliminary section and 58 two-move, 46 three-move, and 8 four-move problems composed by 27 outstanding American problem creators in the last 30 years. Explanation of all terms and exhaustive index. "Just what is wanted for the student," Brian Harley. 112 problems, solutions. vi + 171pp. 5⅜ x 8. 20748-X Paperbound $1.50

AN INTRODUCTION TO THE GEOMETRY OF N DIMENSIONS,
D. H. Y. Sommerville
An introduction presupposing no prior knowledge of the field, the only book in English devoted exclusively to higher dimensional geometry. Discusses fundamental ideas of incidence, parallelism, perpendicularity, angles between linear space; enumerative geometry; analytical geometry from projective and metric points of view; polytopes; elementary ideas in analysis situs; content of hyper-spacial figures. Bibliography. Index. 60 diagrams. 196pp. 5⅜ x 8.
60494-2 Paperbound $1.50

ELEMENTARY CONCEPTS OF TOPOLOGY, *P. Alexandroff*
First English translation of the famous brief introduction to topology for the beginner or for the mathematician not undertaking extensive study. This unusually useful intuitive approach deals primarily with the concepts of complex, cycle, and homology, and is wholly consistent with current investigations. Ranges from basic concepts of set-theoretic topology to the concept of Betti groups. "Glowing example of harmony between intuition and thought," David Hilbert. Translated by A. E. Farley. Introduction by D. Hilbert. Index. 25 figures. 73pp. 5⅜ x 8.
60747-X Paperbound $1.25

ELEMENTS OF NON-EUCLIDEAN GEOMETRY,
D. M. Y. Sommerville
Unique in proceeding step-by-step, in the manner of traditional geometry. Enables the student with only a good knowledge of high school algebra and geometry to grasp elementary hyperbolic, elliptic, analytic non-Euclidean geometries; space curvature and its philosophical implications; theory of radical axes; homothetic centres and systems of circles; parataxy and parallelism; absolute measure; Gauss' proof of the defect area theorem; geodesic representation; much more, all with exceptional clarity. 126 problems at chapter endings provide progressive practice and familiarity. 133 figures. Index. xvi + 274pp. 5⅜ x 8.
60460-8 Paperbound $2.00

INTRODUCTION TO THE THEORY OF NUMBERS, *L. E. Dickson*
Thorough, comprehensive approach with adequate coverage of classical literature, an introductory volume beginners can follow. Chapters on divisibility, congruences, quadratic residues & reciprocity. Diophantine equations, etc. Full treatment of binary quadratic forms without usual restriction to integral coefficients. Covers infinitude of primes, least residues. Fermat's theorem. Euler's phi function, Legendre's symbol, Gauss's lemma, automorphs, reduced forms, recent theorems of Thue & Siegel, many more. Much material not readily available elsewhere. 239 problems. Index. I figure. viii + 183pp. 5⅜ x 8.
60342-3 Paperbound $1.75

MATHEMATICAL TABLES AND FORMULAS,
compiled by Robert D. Carmichael and Edwin R. Smith
Valuable collection for students, etc. Contains all tables necessary in college algebra and trigonometry, such as five-place common logarithms, logarithmic sines and tangents of small angles, logarithmic trigonometric functions, natural trigonometric functions, four-place antilogarithms, tables for changing from sexagesimal to circular and from circular to sexagesimal measure of angles, etc. Also many tables and formulas not ordinarily accessible, including powers, roots, and reciprocals, exponential and hyperbolic functions, ten-place logarithms of prime numbers, and formulas and theorems from analytical and elementary geometry and from calculus. Explanatory introduction. viii + 269pp. 5⅜ x 8½.
60111-0 Paperbound $1.50

PRINCIPLES OF STRATIGRAPHY,
A. W. Grabau
Classic of 20th century geology, unmatched in scope and comprehensiveness. Nearly 600 pages cover the structure and origins of every kind of sedimentary, hydrogenic, oceanic, pyroclastic, atmoclastic, hydroclastic, marine hydroclastic, and bioclastic rock; metamorphism; erosion; etc. Includes also the constitution of the atmosphere; morphology of oceans, rivers, glaciers; volcanic activities; faults and earthquakes; and fundamental principles of paleontology (nearly 200 pages). New introduction by Prof. M. Kay, Columbia U. 1277 bibliographical entries. 264 diagrams. Tables, maps, etc. Two volume set. Total of xxxii + 1185pp. 5⅜ x 8. 60686-4, 60687-2 Two volume set, paperbound $6.25

SNOW CRYSTALS, *W. A. Bentley and W. J. Humphreys*
Over 200 pages of Bentley's famous microphotographs of snow flakes—the product of painstaking, methodical work at his Jericho, Vermont studio. The pictures, which also include plates of frost, glaze and dew on vegetation, spider webs, windowpanes; sleet; graupel or soft hail, were chosen both for their scientific interest and their aesthetic qualities. The wonder of nature's diversity is exhibited in the intricate, beautiful patterns of the snow flakes. Introductory text by W. J. Humphreys. Selected bibliography. 2,453 illustrations. 224pp. 8 x 10¼. 20287-9 Paperbound $3.25

THE BIRTH AND DEVELOPMENT OF THE GEOLOGICAL SCIENCES,
F. D. Adams
Most thorough history of the earth sciences ever written. Geological thought from earliest times to the end of the 19th century, covering over 300 early thinkers & systems: fossils & their explanation, vulcanists vs. neptunists, figured stones & paleontology, generation of stones, dozens of similar topics. 91 illustrations, including medieval, renaissance woodcuts, etc. Index. 632 footnotes, mostly bibliographical. 511pp. 5⅜ x 8. 20005-1 Paperbound $2.75

ORGANIC CHEMISTRY, *F. C. Whitmore*
The entire subject of organic chemistry for the practicing chemist and the advanced student. Storehouse of facts, theories, processes found elsewhere only in specialized journals. Covers aliphatic compounds (500 pages on the properties and synthetic preparation of hydrocarbons, halides, proteins, ketones, etc.), alicyclic compounds, aromatic compounds, heterocyclic compounds, organophosphorus and organometallic compounds. Methods of synthetic preparation analyzed critically throughout. Includes much of biochemical interest. "The scope of this volume is astonishing," *Industrial and Engineering Chemistry.* 12,000-reference index. 2387-item bibliography. Total of x + 1005pp. 5⅜ x 8. 60700-3, 60701-1 Two volume set, paperbound $4.50

THE PHASE RULE AND ITS APPLICATION,
Alexander Findlay
Covering chemical phenomena of 1, 2, 3, 4, and multiple component systems, this "standard work on the subject" (*Nature,* London), has been completely revised and brought up to date by A. N. Campbell and N. O. Smith. Brand new material has been added on such matters as binary, tertiary liquid equilibria, solid solutions in ternary systems, quinary systems of salts and water. Completely revised to triangular coordinates in ternary systems, clarified graphic representation, solid models, etc. 9th revised edition. Author, subject indexes. 236 figures. 505 footnotes, mostly bibliographic. xii + 494pp. 5⅜ x 8. 60091-2 Paperbound $2.75

LA BOHEME BY GIACOMO PUCCINI,
translated and introduced by Ellen H. Bleiler
Complete handbook for the operagoer, with everything needed for full enjoyment except the musical score itself. Complete Italian libretto, with new,
modern English line-by-line translation—the only libretto printing all repeats;
biography of Puccini; the librettists; background to the opera, Murger's La
Boheme, etc.; circumstances of composition and performances; plot summary;
and pictorial section of 73 illustrations showing Puccini, famous singers and
performances, etc. Large clear type for easy reading. 124pp. 5⅜ x 8½.
20404-9 Paperbound $1.25

ANTONIO STRADIVARI: HIS LIFE AND WORK (1644-1737),
W. Henry Hill, Arthur F. Hill, and Alfred E. Hill
Still the only book that really delves into life and art of the incomparable
Italian craftsman, maker of the finest musical instruments in the world today.
The authors, expert violin-makers themselves, discuss Stradivari's ancestry, his
construction and finishing techniques, distinguished characteristics of many
of his instruments and their locations. Included, too, is story of introduction
of his instruments into France, England, first revelation of their supreme
merit, and information on his labels, number of instruments made, prices,
mystery of ingredients of his varnish, tone of pre-1684 Stradivari violin and
changes between 1684 and 1690. An extremely interesting, informative account
for all music lovers, from craftsman to concert-goer. Republication of original
(1902) edition. New introduction by Sydney Beck, Head of Rare Book and
Manuscript Collections, Music Division, New York Public Library. Analytical
index by Rembert Wurlitzer. Appendixes. 68 illustrations. 30 full-page plates.
4 in color. xxvi + 315pp. 5⅜ x 8½. 20425-1 Paperbound $2.25

MUSICAL AUTOGRAPHS FROM MONTEVERDI TO HINDEMITH,
Emanuel Winternitz
For beauty, for intrinsic interest, for perspective on the composer's personality,
for subtleties of phrasing, shading, emphasis indicated in the autograph but
suppressed in the printed score, the mss. of musical composition are fascinating
documents which repay close study in many different ways. This 2-volume
work reprints facsimiles of mss. by virtually every major composer, and many
minor figures—196 examples in all. A full text points out what can be learned
from mss., analyzes each sample. Index. Bibliography. 18 figures. 196 plates.
Total of 170pp. of text. 7⅞ x 10¾.
21312-9, 21313-7 Two volume set, paperbound $5.00

J. S. BACH,
Albert Schweitzer
One of the few great full-length studies of Bach's life and work, and the
study upon which Schweitzer's renown as a musicologist rests. On first appearance (1911), revolutionized Bach performance. The only writer on Bach to
be musicologist, performing musician, and student of history, theology and
philosophy, Schweitzer contributes particularly full sections on history of German Protestant church music, theories on motivic pictorial representations
in vocal music, and practical suggestions for performance. Translated by
Ernest Newman. Indexes. 5 illustrations. 650 musical examples. Total of xix
+ 928pp. 5⅜ x 8½. 21631-4, 21632-2 Two volume set, paperbound $4.50

A COURSE IN MATHEMATICAL ANALYSIS,
Edouard Goursat
Trans. by E. R. Hedrick, O. Dunkel, H. G. Bergmann. Classic study of fundamental material thoroughly treated. Extremely lucid exposition of wide range
of subject matter for student with one year of calculus. Vol. 1: Derivatives and
differentials, definite integrals, expansions in series, applications to geometry.
52 figures, 556pp. 60554-X Paperbound $3.00. Vol. 2, Part I: Functions of a
complex variable, conformal representations, doubly periodic functions, natural boundaries, etc. 38 figures, 269pp. 60555-8 Paperbound $2.25. Vol. 2,
Part II: Differential equations, Cauchy-Lipschitz method, nonlinear differential
equations, simultaneous equations, etc. 308pp. 60556-6 Paperbound $2.50.
Vol. 3, Part I: Variation of solutions, partial differential equations of the
second order. 15 figures, 339pp. 61176-0 Paperbound $3.00. Vol. 3, Part II:
Integral equations, calculus of variations. 13 figures, 389pp. 61177-9 Paperbound
$3.00 60554-X, 60555-8, 60556-6 61176-0, 61177-9 Six volume set,
paperbound $13.75

PLANETS, STARS AND GALAXIES,
A. E. Fanning
Descriptive astronomy for beginners; the solar system; neighboring galaxies;
seasons; quasars; fly-by results from Mars, Venus, Moon; radio astronomy; etc.
all simply explained. Revised up to 1966 by author and Prof. D. H. Menzel,
former Director, Harvard College Observatory. 29 photos, 16 figures. 189pp.
5⅜ x 8½.   21680-2 Paperbound $1.50

GREAT IDEAS IN INFORMATION THEORY, LANGUAGE AND CYBERNETICS,
Jagjit Singh
Winner of Unesco's Kalinga Prize covers language, metalanguages, analog and
digital computers, neural systems, work of McCulloch, Pitts, von Neumann,
Turing, other important topics. No advanced mathematics needed, yet a full
discussion without compromise or distortion. 118 figures. ix + 338pp. 5⅜ x 8½.
21694-2 Paperbound $2.25

GEOMETRIC EXERCISES IN PAPER FOLDING,
T. Sundara Row
Regular polygons, circles and other curves can be folded or pricked on paper,
then used to demonstrate geometric propositions, work out proofs, set up well-
known problems. 89 illustrations, photographs of actually folded sheets. xii +
148pp. 5⅜ x 8½.   21594-6 Paperbound $1.00

VISUAL ILLUSIONS, THEIR CAUSES, CHARACTERISTICS AND APPLICATIONS,
M. Luckiesh
The visual process, the structure of the eye, geometric, perspective illusions,
influence of angles, illusions of depth and distance, color illusions, lighting
effects, illusions in nature, special uses in painting, decoration, architecture,
magic, camouflage. New introduction by W. H. Ittleson covers modern developments in this area. 100 illustrations. xxi + 252pp. 5⅜ x 8.
21530-X Paperbound $1.50

ATOMS AND MOLECULES SIMPLY EXPLAINED,
B. C. Saunders and R. E. D. Clark
Introduction to chemical phenomena and their applications: cohesion, particles,
crystals, tailoring big molecules, chemist as architect, with applications in
radioactivity, color photography, synthetics, biochemistry, polymers, and many
other important areas. Non technical. 95 figures. x + 299pp. 5⅜ x 8½.
21282-3 Paperbound $1.50

HEAR ME TALKIN' TO YA, *edited by Nat Shapiro and Nat Hentoff*
In their own words, Louis Armstrong, King Oliver, Fletcher Henderson, Bunk Johnson, Bix Beiderbecke, Billy Holiday, Fats Waller, Jelly Roll Morton, Duke Ellington, and many others comment on the origins of jazz in New Orleans and its growth in Chicago's South Side, Kansas City's jam sessions, Depression Harlem, and the modernism of the West Coast schools. Taken from taped conversations, letters, magazine articles, other first-hand sources. Editors' introduction. xvi + 429pp. 5⅜ x 8½.   21726-4 Paperbound $2.00

THE JOURNAL OF HENRY D. THOREAU
A 25-year record by the great American observer and critic, as complete a record of a great man's inner life as is anywhere available. Thoreau's Journals served him as raw material for his formal pieces, as a place where he could develop his ideas, as an outlet for his interests in wild life and plants, in writing as an art, in classics of literature, Walt Whitman and other contemporaries, in politics, slavery, individual's relation to the State, etc. The Journals present a portrait of a remarkable man, and are an observant social history. Unabridged republication of 1906 edition, Bradford Torrey and Francis H. Allen, editors. Illustrations. Total of 1888pp. 8⅜ x 12¼.
                    20312-3, 20313-1 Two volume set. clothbound $30.00

A SHAKESPEARIAN GRAMMAR, *E. A. Abbott*
Basic reference to Shakespeare and his contemporaries, explaining through thousands of quotations from Shakespeare, Jonson, Beaumont and Fletcher, North's *Plutarch* and other sources the grammatical usage differing from the modern. First published in 1870 and written by a scholar who spent much of his life isolating principles of Elizabethan language, the book is unlikely ever to be superseded. Indexes. xxiv + 511pp. 5⅜ x 8½. 21582-2 Paperbound $3.00

FOLK-LORE OF SHAKESPEARE, *T. F. Thistelton Dyer*
Clàssic study, drawing from Shakespeare a large body of references to supernatural beliefs, terminology of falconry and hunting, games and sports, good luck charms, marriage customs, folk medicines, superstitions about plants, animals, birds, argot of the underworld, sexual slang of London, proverbs, drinking customs, weather lore, and much else. From full compilation comes a mirror of the 17th-century popular mind. Index. ix + 526pp. 5⅜ x 8½.
                            21614-4 Paperbound $2.75

THE NEW VARIORUM SHAKESPEARE, *edited by H. H. Furness*
By far the richest editions of the plays ever produced in any country or language. Each volume contains complete text (usually First Folio) of the play, all variants in Quarto and other Folio texts, editorial changes by every major editor to Furness's own time (1900), footnotes to obscure references or language, extensive quotes from literature of Shakespearian criticism, essays on plot sources (often reprinting sources in full), and much more.

HAMLET, *edited by H. H. Furness*
Total of xxvi + 905pp. 5⅜ x 8½.
                    21004-9, 21005-7 Two volume set, paperbound $5.25
TWELFTH NIGHT, *edited by H. H. Furness*
Index. xxii + 434pp. 5⅜ x 8½.   21189-4 Paperbound $2.75

SOCIAL THOUGHT FROM LORE TO SCIENCE,
H. E. Barnes and H. Becker
An immense survey of sociological thought and ways of viewing, studying, planning, and reforming society from earliest times to the present. Includes thought on society of preliterate peoples, ancient non-Western cultures, and every great movement in Europe, America, and modern Japan. Analyzes hundreds of great thinkers: Plato, Augustine, Bodin, Vico, Montesquieu, Herder, Comte, Marx, etc. Weighs the contributions of utopians, sophists, fascists and communists; economists, jurists, philosophers, ecclesiastics, and every 19th and 20th century school of scientific sociology, anthropology, and social psychology throughout the world. Combines topical, chronological, and regional approaches, treating the evolution of social thought as a process rather than as a series of mere topics. "Impressive accuracy, competence, and discrimination . . . easily the best single survey," *Nation*. Thoroughly revised, with new material up to 1960. 2 indexes. Over 2200 bibliographical notes. Three volume set. Total of 1586pp. 5⅜ x 8.
20901-6, 20902-4, 20903-2 Three volume set, paperbound $9.00

A HISTORY OF HISTORICAL WRITING, *Harry Elmer Barnes*
Virtually the only adequate survey of the whole course of historical writing in a single volume. Surveys developments from the beginnings of historiography in the ancient Near East and the Classical World, up through the Cold War. Covers major historians in detail, shows interrelationship with cultural background, makes clear individual contributions, evaluates and estimates importance; also enormously rich upon minor authors and thinkers who are usually passed over. Packed with scholarship and learning, clear, easily written. Indispensable to every student of history. Revised and enlarged up to 1961. Index and bibliography. xv + 442pp. 5⅜ x 8½.
20104-X Paperbound $2.75

JOHANN SEBASTIAN BACH, *Philipp Spitta*
The complete and unabridged text of the definitive study of Bach. Written some 70 years ago, it is still unsurpassed for its coverage of nearly all aspects of Bach's life and work. There could hardly be a finer non-technical introduction to Bach's music than the detailed, lucid analyses which Spitta provides for hundreds of individual pieces. 26 solid pages are devoted to the B minor mass, for example, and 30 pages to the glorious St. Matthew Passion. This monumental set also includes a major analysis of the music of the 18th century: Buxtehude, Pachelbel, etc. "Unchallenged as the last word on one of the supreme geniuses of music," John Barkham, *Saturday Review Syndicate*. Total of 1819pp. Heavy cloth binding. 5⅜ x 8.
22278-0, 22279-9 Two volume set, clothbound $15.00

BEETHOVEN AND HIS NINE SYMPHONIES, *George Grove*
In this modern middle-level classic of musicology Grove not only analyzes all nine of Beethoven's symphonies very thoroughly in terms of their musical structure, but also discusses the circumstances under which they were written, Beethoven's stylistic development, and much other background material. This is an extremely rich book, yet very easily followed; it is highly recommended to anyone seriously interested in music. Over 250 musical passages. Index. viii + 407pp. 5⅜ x 8.
20334-4 Paperbound $2.25

APPLIED OPTICS AND OPTICAL DESIGN,
A. E. Conrady
With publication of vol. 2, standard work for designers in optics is now complete for first time. Only work of its kind in English; only detailed work for practical designer and self-taught. Requires, for bulk of work, no math above trig. Step-by-step exposition, from fundamental concepts of geometrical, physical optics, to systematic study, design, of almost all types of optical systems. Vol. 1: all ordinary ray-tracing methods; primary aberrations; necessary higher aberration for design of telescopes, low-power microscopes, photographic equipment. Vol. 2: (Completed from author's notes by R. Kingslake, Dir. Optical Design, Eastman Kodak.) Special attention to high-power microscope, anastigmatic photographic objectives. "An indispensable work," *J., Optical Soc. of Amer.* Index. Bibliography. 193 diagrams. 852pp. 6⅛ x 9¼.
60611-2, 60612-0 Two volume set, paperbound $8.00

MECHANICS OF THE GYROSCOPE, THE DYNAMICS OF ROTATION,
R. F. Deimel, Professor of Mechanical Engineering at Stevens Institute of Technology
Elementary general treatment of dynamics of rotation, with special application of gyroscopic phenomena. No knowledge of vectors needed. Velocity of a moving curve, acceleration to a point, general equations of motion, gyroscopic horizon, free gyro, motion of discs, the damped gyro, 103 similar topics. Exercises. 75 figures. 208pp. 5⅜ x 8.
60066-1 Paperbound $1.75

STRENGTH OF MATERIALS,
J. P. Den Hartog
Full, clear treatment of elementary material (tension, torsion, bending, compound stresses, deflection of beams, etc.), plus much advanced material on engineering methods of great practical value: full treatment of the Mohr circle, lucid elementary discussions of the theory of the center of shear and the "Myosotis" method of calculating beam deflections, reinforced concrete, plastic deformations, photoelasticity, etc. In all sections, both general principles and concrete applications are given. Index. 186 figures (160 others in problem section). 350 problems, all with answers. List of formulas. viii + 323pp. 5⅜ x 8.
60755-0 Paperbound $2.50

HYDRAULIC TRANSIENTS,
G. R. Rich
The best text in hydraulics ever printed in English . . . by former Chief Design Engineer for T.V.A. Provides a transition from the basic differential equations of hydraulic transient theory to the arithmetic integration computation required by practicing engineers. Sections cover Water Hammer, Turbine Speed Regulation, Stability of Governing, Water-Hammer Pressures in Pump Discharge Lines, The Differential and Restricted Orifice Surge Tanks, The Normalized Surge Tank Charts of Calame and Gaden, Navigation Locks, Surges in Power Canals—Tidal Harmonics, etc. Revised and enlarged. Author's prefaces. Index. xiv + 409pp. 5⅜ x 8½.
60116-1 Paperbound $2.50

Prices subject to change without notice.

Available at your book dealer or write for free catalogue to Dept. Adsci, Dover Publications, Inc., 180 Varick St., N.Y., N.Y. 10014. Dover publishes more than 150 books each year on science, elementary and advanced mathematics, biology, music, art, literary history, social sciences and other areas.